TEACHING Terrific 4's

TEACHING Terrific 4's and other children

AnaLynn Jones-Sample, Ed.D. Carol Crownover, M.S.
Elizabeth M. Jones, B.S.

Humanics Learning
Lake Worth, FL

Teaching Terrific Fours
A Humanics Learning Publication
© 2013 Second Edition
© 2006 by Brumby Holdings, LLC

No part of this book may be reproduced or transmitted in any form or by any means, electronic or mechanical, including photocopying, recording, or by any information storage and retrieval system, without written permission from the publisher. For information, address Brumby.

Humanics Learning Publications are an imprint of and published by Humanics Publishing Group, a division of Brumby Holdings, LLC. It's trademark, consisting of the words "Humanics Learning" and a portrayal of a silhouetted girl, is registered in the U.S. Patent Office and in other countries.

Brumby Holdings, LLC
12 S. Dixie Hwy.
Ste. 203
Lake Worth, FL 33460

Printed in the United States of America and the United Kingdom

Library of Congress Control Number: 2006929650

ISBN (Paperback): 0-89334-419-2
ISBN (Hardcover): 0-89334-420-6

Contents

Introduction 1
    Design and Implementation of the Activities 5
    School Readiness Guidelines 7
        Cognitive Domains (reading, writing, listening, viewing, speaking,
            mathematics, scientific thinking
    Social/Emotional Development 11
    Physical Development 12
        Gross motor
        Fine motor
    Music and Movement 13
    Letter of the Week 14
    Character Education 28
        Honesty
        Courage
        Gratitude
        Generosity
        Responsibility
        Caring
        Knowledge
        Fairness
        Patriotism
    Classroom Environment 38
        Room arrangement
    Suggestions for Designing Each Interest Area 41
        Dramatic Play Area
        Block Area
        Table Toys or Manipulatives
        Art Area
    Daily Routine 44
    Adult/Child Interaction 47

Literacy Activities 51
   Where the Butterflies Grow 52
   I'm Going to be a Police Officer 53
   Alpha Bears 54
   The Bears Toothache 55
   Chrysanthemum 56
   Humpty Dumpty 57
   If You Give a Mouse a Cookie 58
   I Want to be an Astronaut 59
   Pet Show 60
   Trucks 62
   Harry the Dirty Dog Story Mural 63
   The Snowman 69
   Ira Sleeps Over 70
   The Little Red Hen 71
   A Letter to Amy 73
   Gone Fishing 74
   Have You Seen Bugs 80
   Clifford's Birthday Party 82
   I Am Me 84
   The Kissing Hand 86
   The Grouchy Ladybug 88
   There's an Alligator Under My Bed 91
   The Very Hungry Caterpillar 92
   Mary Wore Her Red Dress Henry Wore His Green Sneakers 96
   Here Are My Hands 97
   Twinkle Twinkle Little Star 99

Discovery Activities 101
   A Shape For Me 102
   Tearing A Rainbow 104
   Tear It Up 106
   Shape It Up 108
   Stop, Drop, Roll 111
   Oobleck Activities 113
   Oobleck Recipe 115
   Mouse House 116
   Germy Germs 117

    Eight Germs 119
    Doctor Doctor 122
    Create Your Own Germ 124
    Two Friendly Hands 125
    Cover Your Sneeze 128
    Cleared for Landing 130
    Astronaut Training Center 132
    Big Small, Big Small 134
    I Can Write 136
    Look What I Can Do Now 138
    Our Favorite Colors 140
    Necklace For My Secret Pal 142
    Share A Brush 145
    Invent an Insect 147
    What's Living In My Pond 149
    Musical Share-A-Chair 151
    Look At Beautiful Me 152
    Little Boy Blue 155
    Let It Melt 158
    Healthy Apples 160
    Fruit and Vegetable Bingo 164
    Let's Eat Out 175

Appendices **177**
    Appendix I: Letter Appendix 179
    Appendix II: Activity Compliance with Pre-K Standards .233
    Appendix III: Common Core Standards Correlations 257

About the Authors **261**

Introduction

Introduction

When we were approached to write a book entitled, "Teaching Terrific Four's" we were filled with enthusiasm and excitement. Four-year-old children are so full of wonder. The world is theirs to explore and with the proper nurturing they can accomplish many great things.

In a typical preschool class, there will be four-year-olds at several different levels of development. It is important for the preschool teacher to provide activities that meet the needs of all children, that all children can accomplish with success, and that can help to move them to higher levels of development.

This book is designed to assist early childhood educators in implementing literacy and other developmentally appropriate cognitive, social and emotional, as well as fine and gross motor activities.

Research has proven that a four-year-old experience is perhaps the most important year in a child's life as it pertains to readiness to enter kindergarten.

Each activity in the book has been "tried and tested" by colleagues; those who teach in a Pre-K four program. We hope you enjoy seeing the delight in these young learners as they embark on a fascinating, wondrous stage of development.

Design and Implementation of the Activities

This book is organized into thematic units appropriate for four-year-old children. The activities are designed to meet cognitive, social/emotional, and physical standards for children of this age group.

The book is divided into chapters that include:

- Readiness guidelines for four-year-olds.

- Discovery Activities—Hands-on activities that will help build cognitive and problem-solving skills.

- Literacy Activities—Theme-based activities that incorporate a variety of literature along with activities to enhance vocabulary and language development.

- Character Education—Developmentally appropriate activities for building good citizenship are provided.

- Letter of the week activities—Reproducible letters and guidelines for daily implementation and a variety of fun ideas for teaching letter recognition and beginning letter sounds.

- Classroom environment—Strategies for room arrangement, daily routine, and adult-child interactions that will set the tone for a positive learning experience.

When used together, these activities will prepare students to enter Kindergarten with the knowledge and skills necessary to be successful in school. Discover how these activities will thrill young learners while meeting state and national standards!

School Readiness Guidelines

Cognitive Domains

READING:

- Uses book title and pictures to predict the meaning of the story.

- Attaches meaning to visual symbols.

- Retells stories, songs, and finger plays in sequence.

- Selects materials to read for pleasure.

- Identifies characters and/or items that belong in the story after the story is read.

- Uses classroom charts and non-fiction picture books to obtain information; uses pictures, signs, graphs, charts.

WRITING:

- Dictates and draws main ideas of a concept.

- Role plays.

- Writes and/or draws in various ways (scribbles, uses letter-like forms and letters, attempts to copy text).

- Makes predictions about classroom activities.

- Uses components of the computer/keyboard and mouse.

- Describes steps in sequence for simple tasks (ex. caring for pet, cleaning house and work areas, etc.).

7

LISTENING, VIEWING, AND SPEAKING:

- Follows short, simple directions (ex. classroom procedures/activities).

- Chooses to listen to materials in classroom listening center.

- Engages in conversation to seek answers or gain further explanation of another's ideas.

- Responds to and uses body language cues such as eye contact, smiles, and simple hand gestures.

- Speaks clearly and audibly during large and small group situations.

- Asks questions to seek further explanations of other people's ideas.

- Speaks effectively in conversation with others.

- Uses words to express one's feelings and/or to meet one's needs.

- Identifies personally meaningful environmental print such as stop signs, fast food restaurant signs, cereal boxes, etc.

- Compares/contrasts personal experiences with those presented in story.

MATHEMATICS:

- Begins to associate the names of some numerals 1-10.

- Using groups of objects, can determine which has more/less and same.

- Uses manipulatives and real objects to show 1:1 correspondence.

- Correctly counts up to at least 10 objects.

- Begins to demonstrate patterns by clapping, moving, and with use of manipulatives.

- Makes comparative judgments (ex. longer/shorter, larger/smaller, etc.).

- Measures items with non-standard units such as unifix cubes, blocks, thumbs, hands, paperclips, etc.

- Arranges 2-3 items in graduated order using a characteristic such as size, texture, shade of color.

- Explores scales to measure weight; uses ruler or tape measure to measure length.

- Sorts circles, squares, and triangles into their like groups.

- Follows directions to demonstrate "behind, next to, in front of."

- Sorts unit blocks according to shape and label on a shelf.

- Sorts items according to color, shape, and/or size.

- Identifies colors.

- Identifies circle, square, triangle, rectangle, oval.

- Describes a variety of classification schemes and patterns related to sensory attributes (rhythm and sound).

- Describes a variety of classification schemes and patterns related to shapes, colors, numbers.

- Describes a variety of classification schemes and patterns related to similar objects and similar events.

SCIENTIFIC THINKING

- Uses pictures or real objects to create charts or graphs to interpret information and make comparisons such as weather, ways to get home, number of boys/girls, etc.

- Investigates properties and compares materials in the classroom such as items that float or sink, magnetic vs. non-magnetic, etc.

Social-Emotional Development

- Expresses a choice using a sentence.

- Makes a plan with one or more details.

- Attempts at least two ways to solve a problem with materials.

- Engages in pretend play.

- Joins in with one or more child(ren) during play.

- Accomplishes all parts of self-care activity.

- Demonstrates interest and participates in classroom activities.

- Demonstrates a willingness to share materials with another child.

- Initiates and sustains interactions with others (adult and child).

- Accepts responsibility for maintaining the classroom environment.

- Requests adult help in resolving conflicts with another child or is able to negotiate the resolution in a conflict with another child.

- Represents an emotion through pretend play and/or art.

- Identifies an emotion and gives a reason for it.

- Respects the rights of others.

Physical Development

GROSS MOTOR:

- Walks up and down stairs using alternating feet.
- Runs, gallops, jumps with control and is able to stop without falling.
- Throws an object in an intended direction.
- Kicks a ball in an intended direction.
- Catches a beanbag.
- Climbs and slides on playground equipment.

FINE MOTOR:

- Uses small muscles to complete a task (pushing cookie cutter into dough, pulling marker caps off and snapping them back on, connects or snaps manipulatives).
- Uses eye-hand coordination to complete a task (zipping jacket, cutting on a line, dressing dolls, putting puzzles together by matching colors and shapes of pieces).
- Shows beginning control of writing, drawing, and art tools (holding pencil using pincer grasp, etc.).

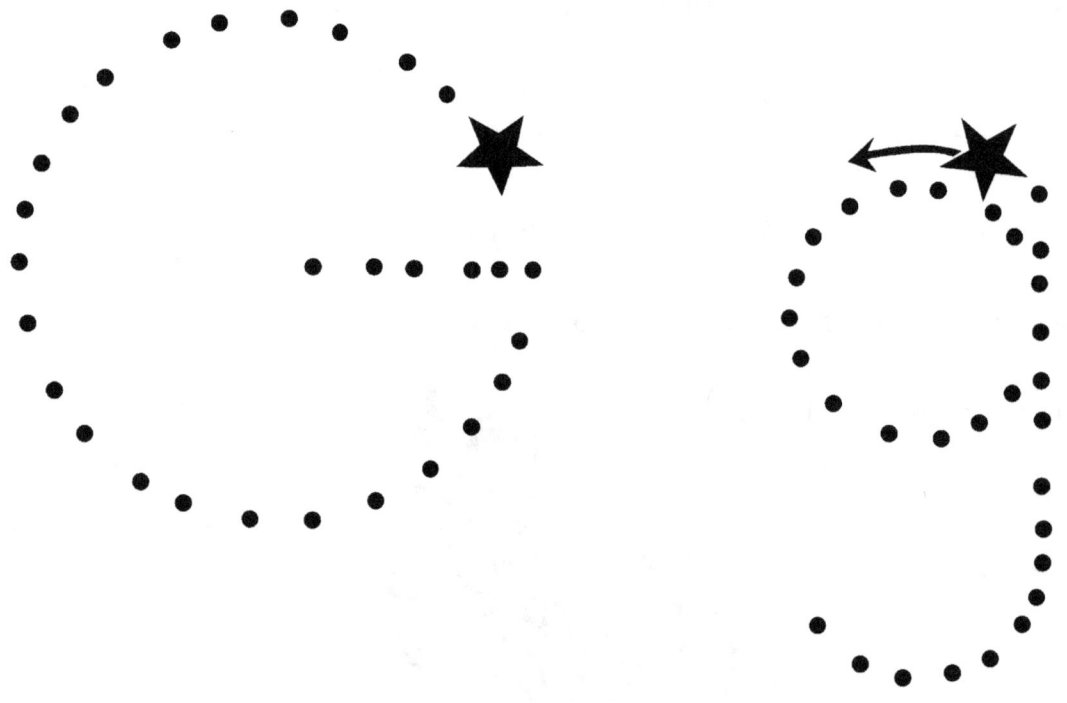

12

Music and Movement

- Participates in musical activities such as dancing, singing, marching.
- Claps or taps sticks to the steady beat of music.
- Copies the clapping beat of the teacher.

Letter of the Week

Research has shown that children who start school with some knowledge of letters and their sounds, have more success in learning to read.

Letter of the week activities should follow these suggested guidelines:

• They should be fun.

• The letters should be cut out by adults, not by children. This activity is designed to focus on letter recognition and not cutting skills. Children need to see the letter cut out properly.

• The activity should include a variety of "hands-on" materials. For example, if an activity calls for gluing yellow items on the letter "Y" provide (yellow) yarn, pipe cleaners, tissue paper, cotton balls, etc.

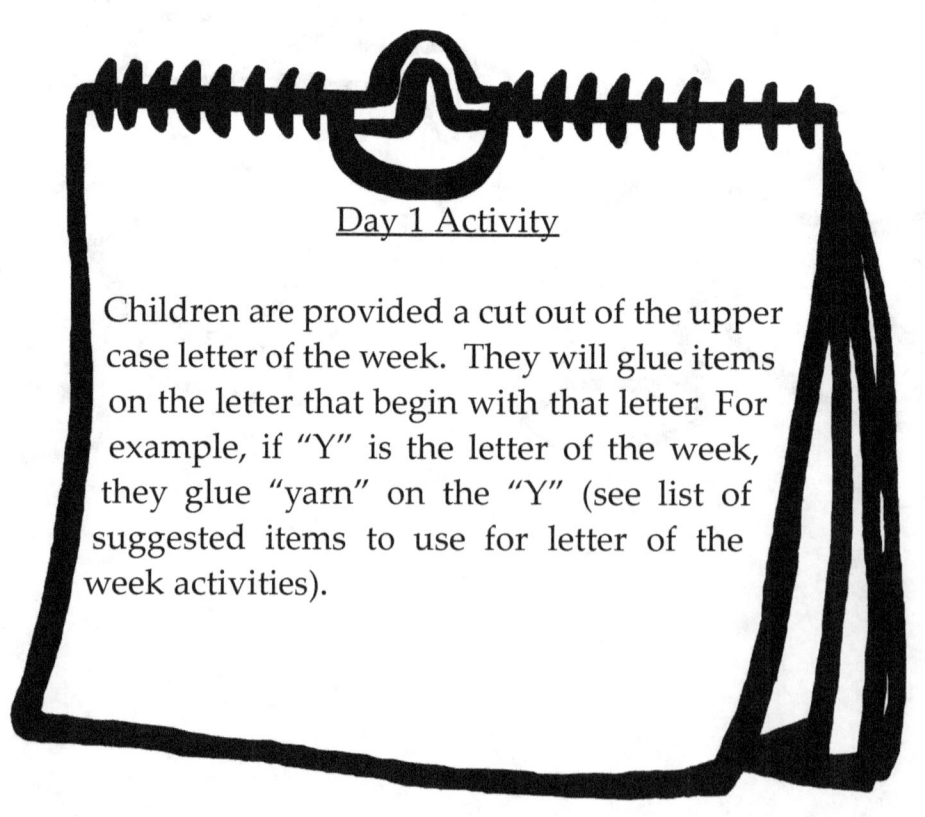

Day 1 Activity

Children are provided a cut out of the upper case letter of the week. They will glue items on the letter that begin with that letter. For example, if "Y" is the letter of the week, they glue "yarn" on the "Y" (see list of suggested items to use for letter of the week activities).

Day 2 Activity

Children are provided a cut out of the lower case letter of the week. They glue items on the letter that begin with that letter (same as day 1 activity, but with the lower case letter).

Day 3 Activity

Children are provided a large letter (approximately 4" tall) drawn by the teacher on a sheet of paper (do not cut out the letter). Provide an upper case and lower case letter of the "letter of the week." Children use "Wikki Sticks" to stick on top of the letter ("Wikki Sticks" are stickable, bendable pipe cleaners, available in most early childhood catalogs. They can be reused throughout the year).

Day 4 Activity

Children go on a "letter search." They are to find the letter of the week in a variety of literature (ex. poems, stories, labels in the classroom, magazines, catalogs, newspapers, etc.) and around the school/center.

Day 5 Activity

Children can trace a teacher-made "dot-to-dot" of the letter of the week. Place the letter at the top of a page (8.5 x 11 inch sheet of paper) and make a dot-to-dot (upper and lower case). Children trace over the letter using finger paint and one finger. Children draw a picture(s) of something that begins with that letter.

Suggested Items to use for Letter of the Week Activities

A a	apples (made from fingerprints, paint)	animals (use various pictures from magazines, or animal stamps or create "finger print" animal pictures)
B b	blue items	brown items
C c	cotton balls	crayons (children decorate their "c" with a variety of different colored crayons)
D d	dots	diamonds (paper diamond shapes or jewels)
E e	elephant (picture)	eggs (children decorate small ovals)
F f	feathers	fish
G g	green things	glue (use glue to make glue dots on the letter "g")
H h	tiny hearts	holes (children use hole punchers to make holes in the letter "h")
I i	ice cream cones	ink (use stamps to stamp on the letter)
J j	jets (picture)	jewels
K k	kangaroo (picture)	kites (small diamond shapes turned into kites)
L l	leaves	lollipops (students draw)
M m	macaroni	mouse (make from thumbprint)

N	n	noodles	number nine (printed on their letter N)
O	o	orange things	orange gelatin mix (place a small amount of glue on the letter; sprinkle with orange gelatin powder)
P	p	paper (use scraps to glue on the letter)	pink items
Q	q	quarters (picture)	question marks
R	r	red items	rice
S	s	sand (glue on letter)	sequins
T	t	teddy bears	tape (children use transparent or masking tape)
U	u	unicorns (picture)	umbrellas (glue half circles to the letter; add a handle to make an umbrella)
V	v	violet things	violin (picture)
W	w	worms	watercolors (children watercolor paint different colors on their W.)
X	x	x-ray (picture)	patterns of x's (XxXxXx) students draw on the letter
Y	y	yarn	yellow things
Z	z	zebra stripes (painted black and white stripes)	zig-zag lines (drawn on by the students)

Use the following pages as cut-outs for your letters of the week.

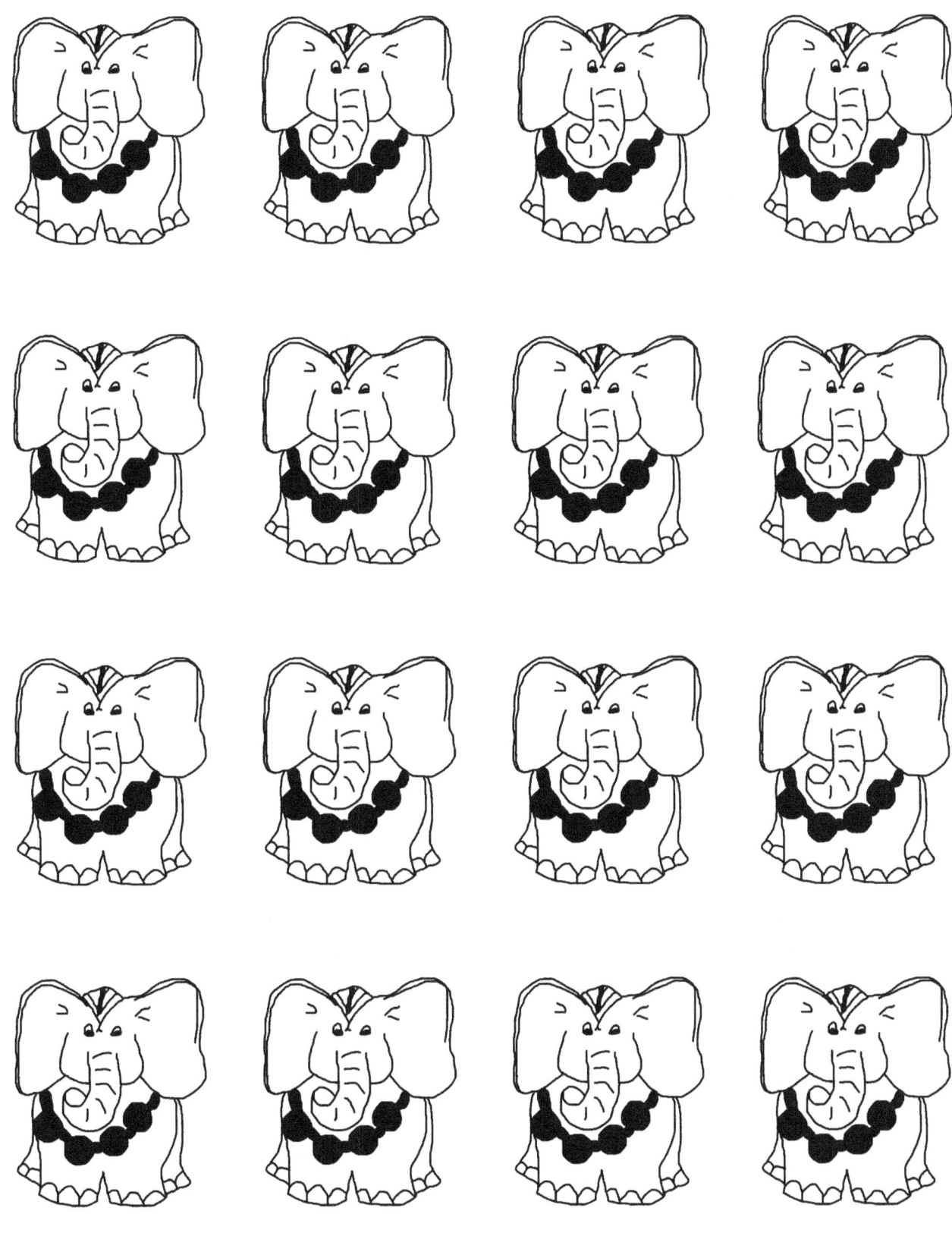

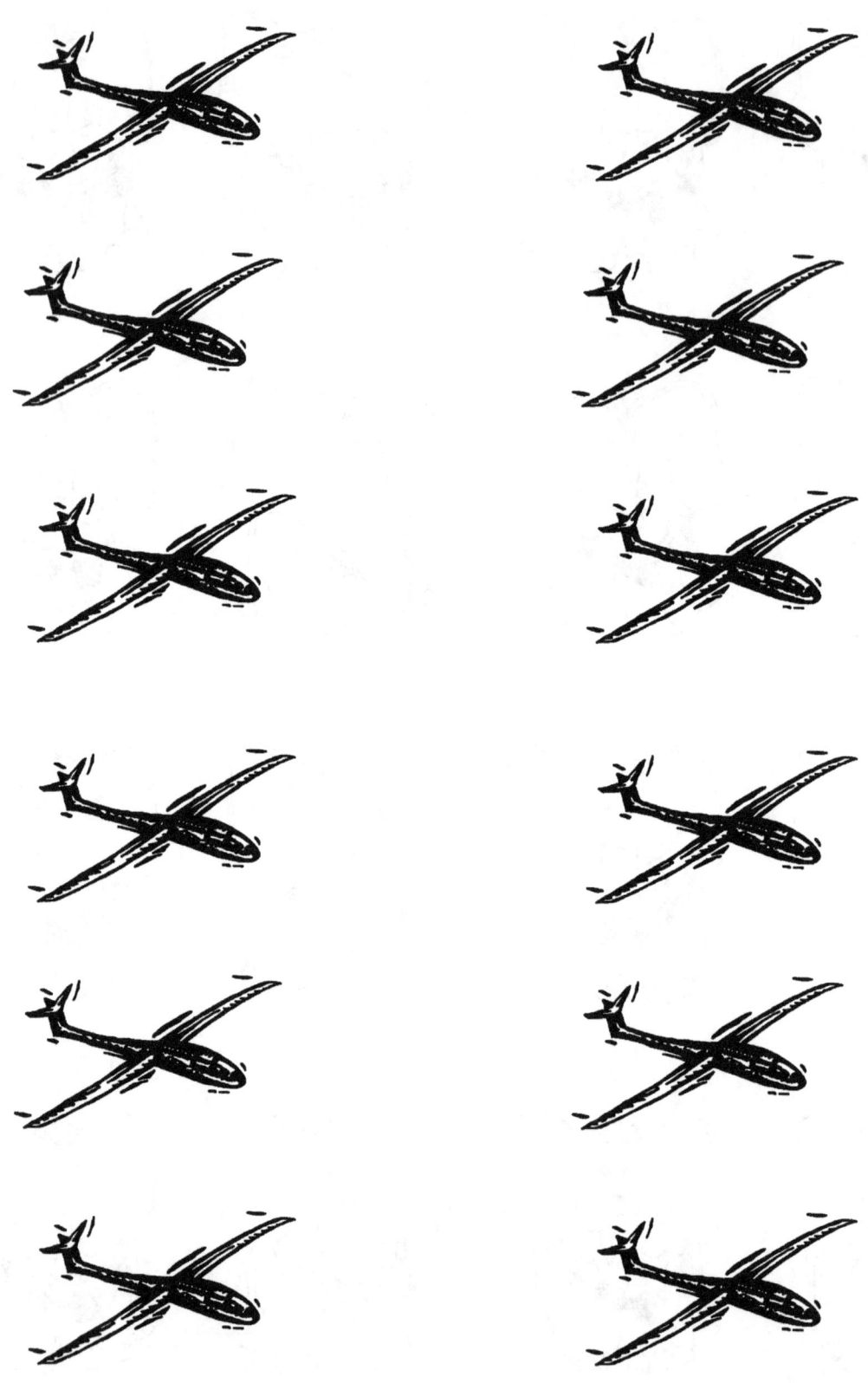

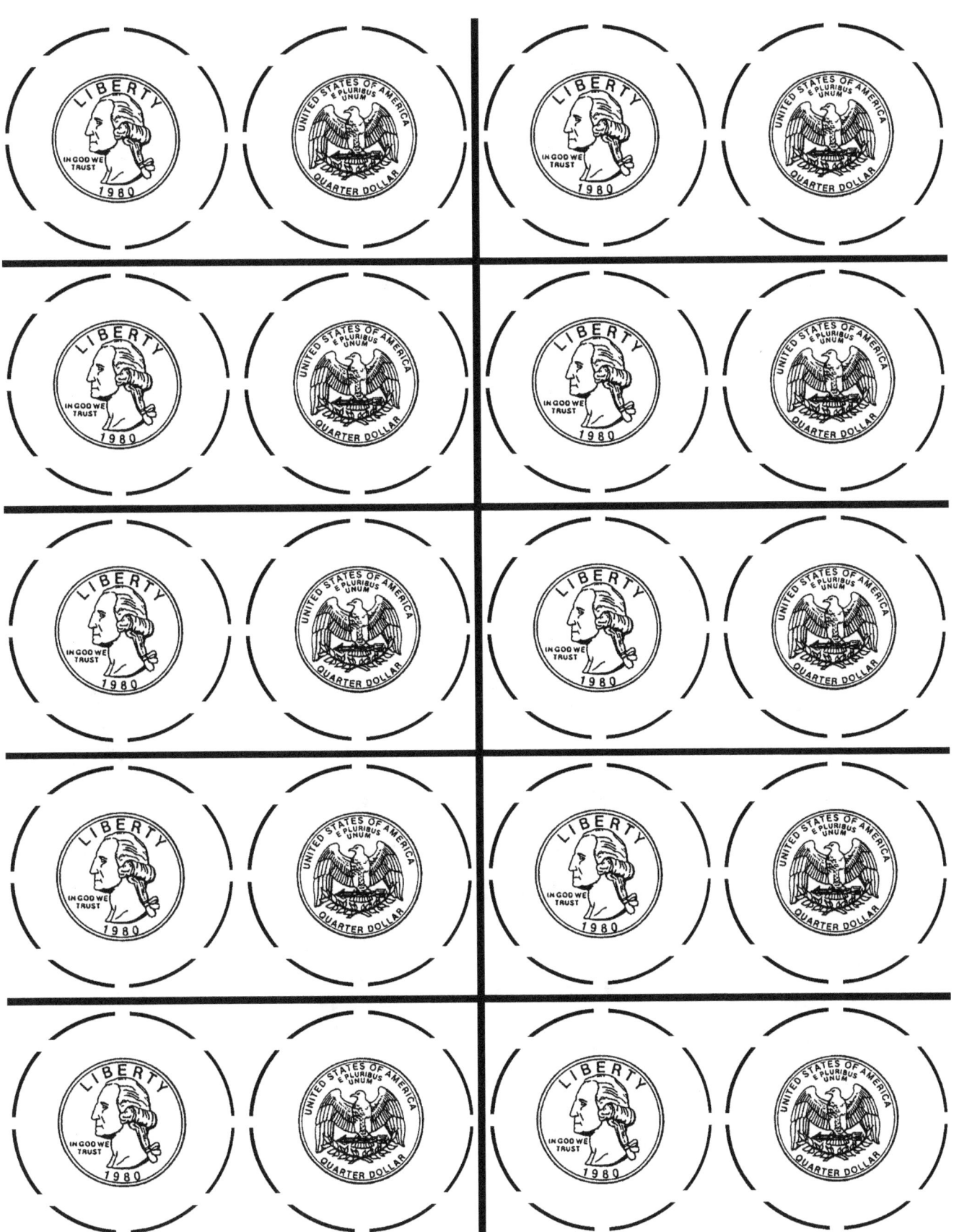

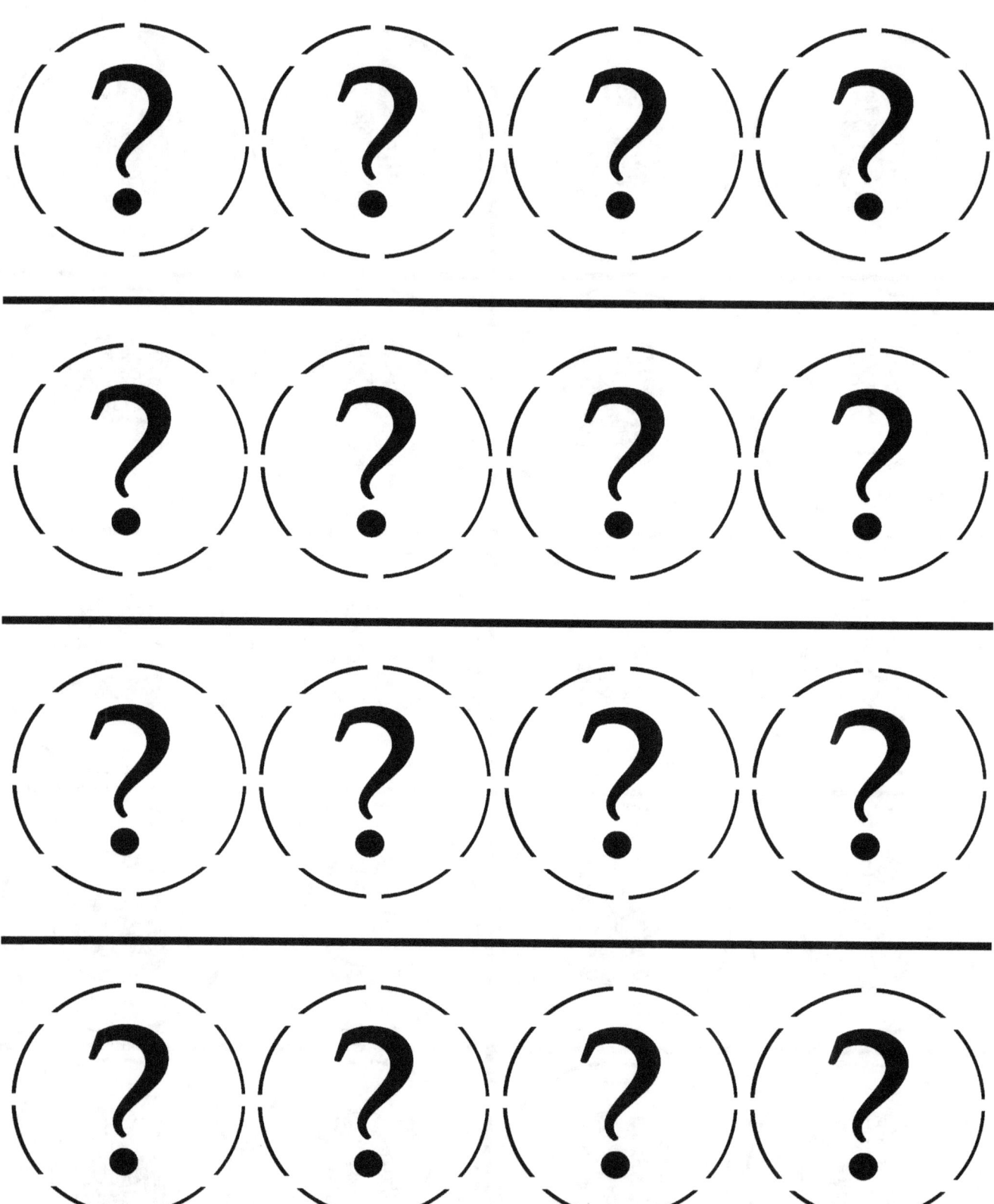

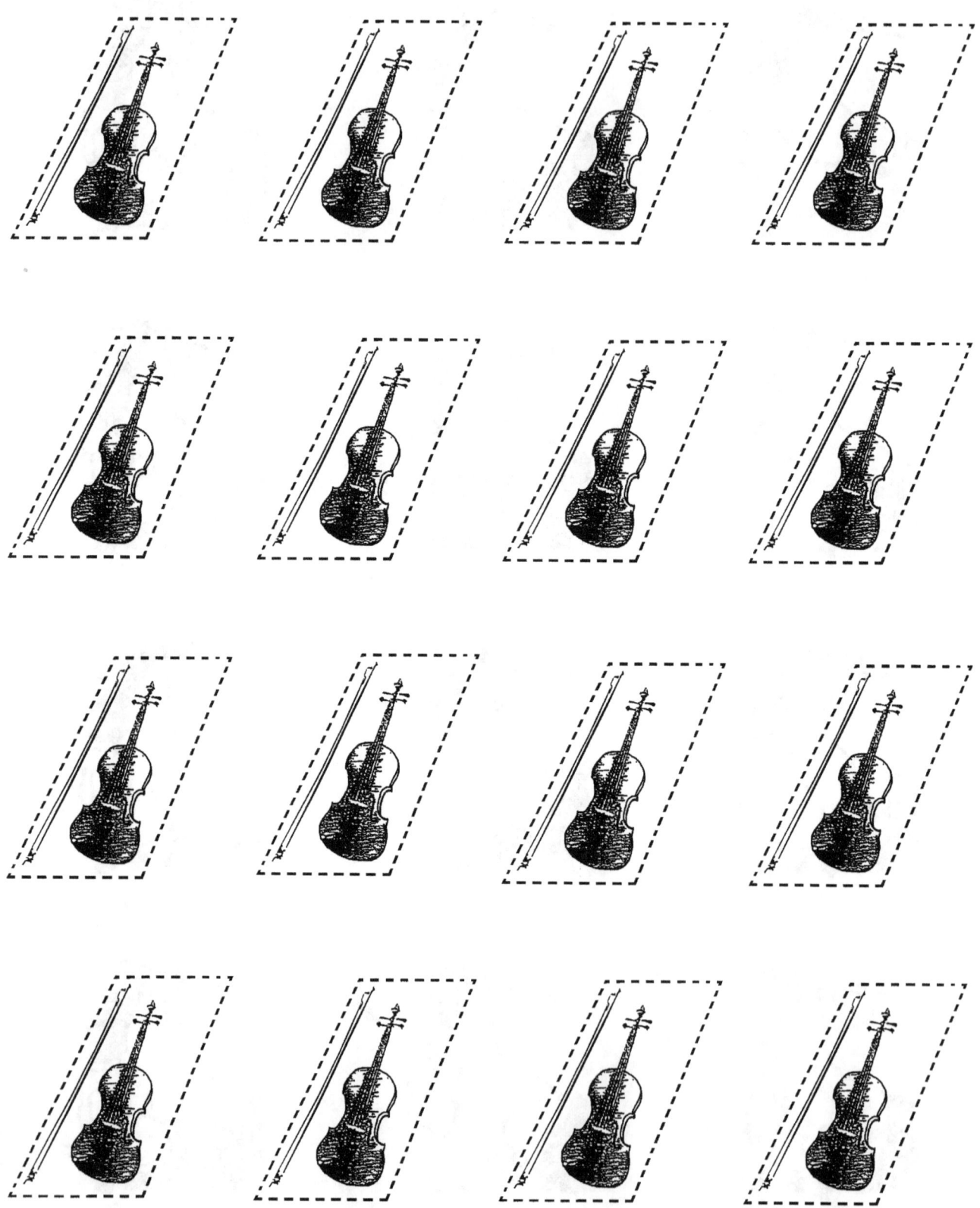

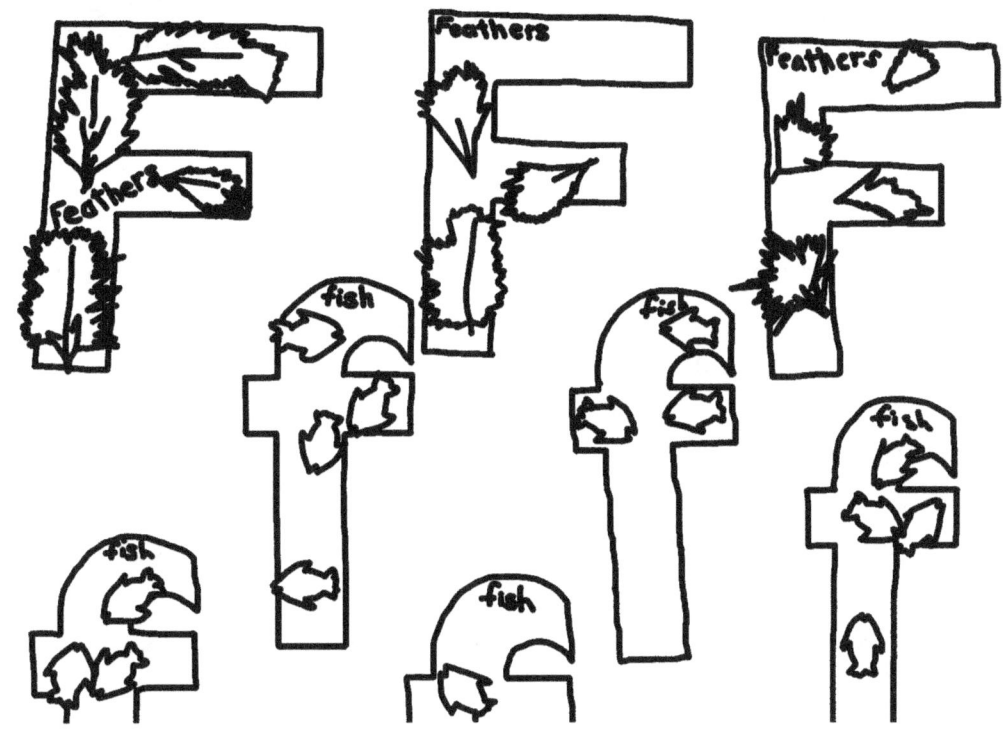

Examples of "Letter of the week."

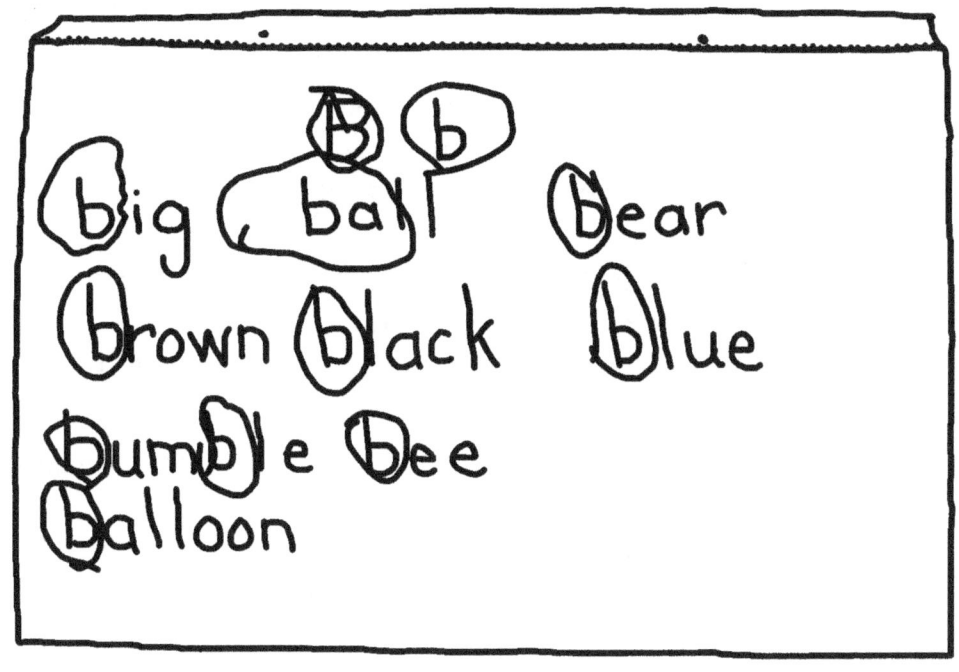

Character Education

RESPECT

- Learning classmate's names is a way to show respect. Pass a heart around the circle. As each child receives the heart, he states his name (some may be shy and will require your assistance. Don't force anyone to speak).
- Ask, "What are your teachers' names?"
- Ask if anyone knows the name of his or her school.
- We show respect by taking care of our classroom. Ask, "How can we help take care of our classroom?"
- Discuss that children should show respect by asking if they may use the toy, rather than taking it from a friend.
- Using kind words with each other is a way to show respect. Ask for a few examples of kind words (ex. "May I use that toy when you are finished?").
- Ask for 2-3 volunteers to share how a friend has been kind and respectful.
- Explain that as we walk through the school/center, being quiet so others can do their work is respectful.
- Explain that using materials the way they are intended is respectful (ex. holding a book, turning pages carefully).
- Explain that calling our parents mom/dad, mama/papa is being respectful. Ask, "What other words do we use when talking to our parents?"
- Ask for 2-3 volunteers to describe how they are respectful at home.
- Ask, "If a visitor enters our room, what would be a respectful thing to do?"
- Ask, "If your teacher is talking to someone, and you need her help right away, what should you say or do?"
- Discuss ways to be respectful to a new student entering our classroom for the first time.
- Discuss and role-play the following scenario: "If someone was sitting a bit too closely, making you feel 'squished,' what could you do, in a respectful way?"

HONESTY

- Ask, "What does it mean to tell the truth?"
- Ask, "If you accidentally broke a glass and your mother asked you what happened, what would you do?"
- Ask, "How would you feel if a friend came over to play and then took your favorite toy home, without asking your permission?"
- Discuss the importance of being honest at a store (ex. if you want something you have to pay for it).
- Ask for 2-3 examples of something that could really happen, and then something "make-believe."
- Provide real and make-believe statements. Ask the children if this could really happen (ex. the dog cooked dinner; the dog ate my sandwich).
- Ask children to help you make up a short story about a child who wanted a toy that someone else had. Ask, "What are some honest ways to go about getting the toy?"
- Ask, "What would you do if you found $1.00 on the classroom floor?" Have a few children act out the scenario.
- Ask for a few volunteers to be honest and tell about something they like about school.
- Act out and discuss the following scenario: Joe was playing with a truck. Ann took the truck from Joe. The two began to argue over the truck. The teacher asked who had it first. Ann says that she did. What should she have said?
- Ask, "What would you do if you saw your friend take a toy from the classroom and put it in his/her back pack?"
- Ask, "Would it be honest to call 9-1-1 to report a fire, if there was no fire?"
- Discuss the importance of being honest if you ever have to call 9-1-1. Why would you call? What would you say?
- Ask someone to tell you something that could really happen, and someone to tell you something that could not really happen (real vs. make-believe).
- Ask the children to answer the following question: "Did you brush your teeth today?"

COURAGE

- Explain that the word courage means being brave. Share a time when you had to be brave (through a bad storm, etc.).
- Ask children if they remember how they felt when they first came to school. Explain that coming to school, for the first time, is a brave thing to do.
- Briefly discuss "stranger danger." Ask the children what a stranger is. Ask, "What should you do if a stranger offers you candy?"
- Discuss the following scenario: You see a classmate fall off the swing. The friend is holding his head and crying. What should you do? Explain that it takes courage to call a teacher for help.
- Ask the children if they can think of some jobs that require workers to have courage (police officer, fire-fighters, tree-cutters, builders, etc.).

- Discuss how storms can be frightening. Ask, "How did your families show they were brave through storms?" (could be snow storms, hurricanes, etc.).
- Ask children about their fears. What are some things that frighten them?
- Ask children to share something they did that required them to have courage.
- Use 3 dolls and act out a scenario in which one doll is being bullied or teased by another. Let the 3rd doll "stick up" for the one being teased. Explain that the doll who helped her friend showed courage.
- Ask for a few volunteers to describe a time when they had courage, or were feeling brave.
- Ask, "Do you know anyone who has been brave, showing courage? How was that person brave?"

GRATITUDE

- Explain that gratitude is like thankfulness. Share something about the class for which you are thankful (ex. I am thankful that everyone knows how to follow the rules).
- Ask children to share something about school for which they are grateful.
- Ask the children why they should be thankful for farmers.
- Ask, "Are you thankful for your families?"
- Remind children about the school/center workers. Tell them you are thankful for custodians, cafeteria workers, etc. Ask if they know why you are thankful for these people.
- Tell children you are thankful for good health. Explain that sometimes you may catch a cold or have a stomachache, but you are strong enough to get well. For that, you are thankful.
- Ask volunteers to tell about one thing at school for which they are grateful.

- Explain that not all children around the world have the chance to go to school. Tell them how grateful you are that they are in your class each day.
- Explain that you are grateful for the use of your hands. Without hands you could not hold a book, draw pictures, hold hands with a friend, or clap for a job well done.
- Explain to the children that you are grateful for your eyes. Ask if anyone knows why.
- Tell children you are thankful for your family. Describe one fun activity that you do with your family. Ask how they have fun with their families (ask for 2-3 volunteers).
- Ask, "Are you thankful for your parents?"
- What are some smells that you are thankful for (favorite foods cooking, flowers, the beach, etc.)?
- Discuss why you are grateful for your ears. How can our ears help us?
- Tell the children you are thankful for the way they know how to follow the rules.

GENEROSITY

- Tell the class that when they share a toy with a friend, they are being generous.
- Ask the children how they feel when someone shares with them.
- Tell the children how much you enjoy giving gifts to the special people in your family.
- Ask the children how they feel when they receive a gift from someone.
- Have two children role play the following: One child is playing with a pegboard and pegs, and the other wants to play, too. What could she say to the friend playing with the pegboard?
- Discuss different ways people in the school/center have been generous to the class (ex. donating time, materials, etc.).
- Ask children to share ways they have been generous to family members (ex. shared toys with siblings).
- Ask the children to identify ways they can be generous to a friend who is feeling sad and lonely.
- Ask, "What should you do or say if someone gives you a gift?"

RESPONSIBILITY

- Tell the children it is their responsibility to do their "class job" each day.
- Share some of your responsibilities with the children: to keep them safe, help them learn important things for kindergarten, cook and feed your families, etc.
- Discuss the responsibilities of some of the school workers or community helpers.
- Discuss the following, using dolls: Two children are building in block area, and they decide to move to the art area. Whose responsibility is it to put the blocks away?
- Discuss some of their "school" responsibilities such as following directions, trying to open food containers, packing back packs, putting toys away, etc.
- Discuss ways we need to be responsible outside: Do not litter, don't waste water, etc.
- Ask the children what would happen if we stopped being responsible for our classroom.
- Discuss ways the children can be responsible at home (ex. clean up toys, take out trash, empty back packs, etc.).
- Ask, "How can you help a friend that is sad?"
- Ask, "How do you feel when someone tells you you've done a good job?"
- Ask, "What are some of your favorite jobs at school/in the classroom?"
- Ask, "Why are covering our coughs and washing our hands important responsibilities?"
- Explain that it is our responsibility to stay quiet when walking through the school/center.
- Discuss the following: If you were with your friend and he or she fell off the swing and got hurt, how could you be a responsible friend?
- Discuss the following: You spilled some glue on the table during work time. Who is responsible for wiping up the spill?

CARING

- Tell children that as they listen closely to you during story time, or other times, they are being "caring" students.
- Ask, "Who are some caring people in the school/center? How do they show they care?"
- Ask, "What are some ways we can be caring to our friends at school?"
- Ask, "What would be a caring thing to say to someone who fell down?"
- Discuss ways to be caring to a new friend who has come to our class for the very first time.
- Ask, "What is a caring thing to say to someone who is sick?"
- Ask, "What is a caring way to handle your cough or sneeze?"
- Ask for examples of how the children are caring to different family members.
- Ask, "How can you tell that your teacher cares about you?"
- Ask, "Why do you think we have class rules (ex. walking feet, kind hands, etc.)?"
- Ask the children to share some of their parents' rules, which show that their parents care about them.
- Ask the children if anyone has a pet. Ask, " How do you show your pet you care for him? How does he show you that he cares for you?"
- What are some ways children need to care for themselves (eating healthy foods, washing hands, etc.)?
- Discuss the nursery rhyme "Jack and Jill." Ask the children what they could say to Jack and Jill that would be caring.
- Ask, "How were you caring to a friend today or yesterday?"

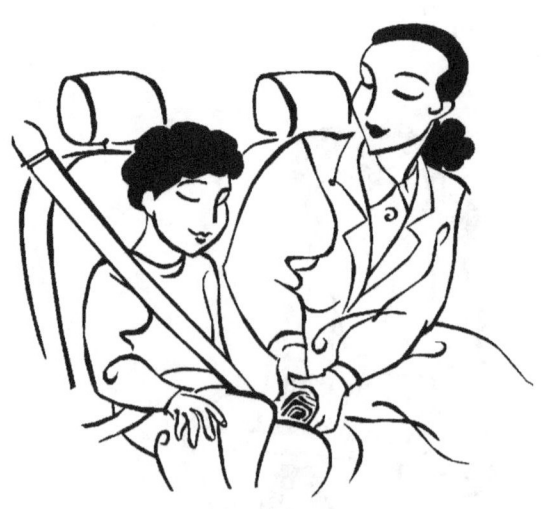

KNOWLEDGE

- Ask children if anyone knows what is meant by knowledge. Explain that it means all that we have learned.
- Ask children to share some of their favorite things that they have learned in school.
- Display a newspaper. Ask, "Why do you think people read the newspaper?" (to learn about the world around them).
- Explain that since being in preschool/Pre-K they have learned many school rules. Ask them to share some of the things they have learned about school.
- Explain that we learn by reading books. Ask, "What other things can we read to learn new information?"
- Explain that all through the day we are learning. Ask, "What is your favorite part of the day? Why?"
- Ask the children, "How do we learn with eyes, ears, nose, hands/skin?" (mouth is excluded because some things should never be put in our mouths).
- Ask, "How can we learn if we like a certain food that we've never had before?"
- Ask, "What are some different ways that adults learn about the world?" (newspaper, television, radio, news).
- Ask, "Of all the ways there are to learn things, what is your favorite way to learn?" (read books? listen to the teacher? try new things? watch television?).
- Ask who has shared some of the things learned at school with people at home.
- Ask children to tell you about some of the things they would like to learn (gain knowledge about what?).

FAIRNESS

- Ask children, "If two friends are arguing over one toy, what is a fair way to settle the argument?"
- Discuss the following: Two children want to write on the chalkboard, but there is only one piece of chalk. What is the fair thing to do? Have two children demonstrate how to be fair in this situation.
- Ask the children, "Why should we put away our toys and materials after we are finished with them? Is it fair to ask someone else to clean up our things?"
- Ask the children, "How are we assigned our class jobs in a fair way?"
- Ask the children, "If there was only one piece of cake left but you and your sister wanted a piece, what would be a fair thing to do?"
- Present the following situation: Line up four dolls and tell the class that you have two cookies (use paper cookies). "What would be a fair way to share two cookies among the four children?"
- Explain that even adults must stand in lines in order to take turns and be fair. In what type of lines must adults wait (ex. grocery story, retail store, restaurant, etc.).
- Ask, "When playing a game, what is a fair way to decide who will go first?" Demonstrate "Eeny, Meeny, Miny, Mo" or 1 Potato, 2 Potato.
- Discuss and demonstrate the following: Your friend takes all the pegs to use for his pegboard, leaving you with none. What could you say to your friend?
- Ask the class if they have ever played a game like "Candy Land" or "Go Fish." How do they feel if another person wins the game? (Children will answer differently depending on their level of development).
- Discuss the following: You are standing in line waiting your turn for the slide. A child pushes in front of you, trying to get to the slide. Is that fair? What could you say to that friend?
- Ask the class, "When we play a game like Duck, Duck, Goose, is it fair to always pick the same friends? How do you feel when you do not get chosen to play games?"
- Ask, "If you found some money would it be fair to keep it?"
- Ask, "Is it fair to play with only a few friends and not play with everyone? What can we do today to be fair during outside time?"

PATRIOTISM

- Ask, "Why do we look at the American flag and say the 'Pledge of Allegiance?'"
- Ask, "What are some ways that we can be good citizens at school?"
- Ask, "If we love our school, would we ever throw trash on the ground?"
- Ask, "Do you know the initials of the United States of American (U.S.A.)?"
- Ask, "Who is the President of the United States?"
- Discuss the word "neighborhood." What is a neighborhood? Explain that when many "neighborhoods" are put together, they form a town.
- Display the American flag. Ask, "What are the colors in the American flag?" (explain that every country has its own special flag).
- Discuss how the class rules help us to be good citizens. Ask, "What rules do adults have to follow?"
- Discuss differences among people. Look around the room. Notice differences in eye color, hair color, clothes, likes and dislikes. Tell the children that while we are all different we still all work together to form a wonderful classroom of students.
- Ask, "Why do you think our school/center has an American flag outside?"
- Explain that when we love our country, we are being "patriotic." Ask, "What do you love about where you live?"
- Tell the children that our country has a birthday and it is July the 4th. Tell them that our country is over 200 years old.
- Display a globe. Explain that some children living in different parts of the world have no schools. Our country provides schools for all children.
- Discuss voting. Tell the children that adults will "vote" for things they want, during an election. Have a class vote on a favorite class activity (use the daily routine cards).
- Point to the flag. Explain that there is one star for each state and one of those stars is for (your state).

Classroom Environment

The classroom environment contributes greatly to the cognitive, physical, and social-emotional development of children. It is through the classroom environment that each child learns to become an accepted and important member of a group. By manipulating different aspects of the environment, the teacher is able to send specific messages and set a positive tone for learning.

The classroom environment includes the following components: room arrangement, daily routine, and adult-child interactions. Each component must be carefully planned, keeping the needs of the four-year-old children in mind. Careful planning will provide structure, positive momentum, and help prevent behavior problems, while contributing to the overall growth of each child.

Room Arrangement

- The first thing to always consider is the health and safety of the children. Be sure there are no broken toys or furnishings with sharp or protruding edges. Keep all cleaning supplies and other chemicals in a locked storage unit, so that no child can come in contact with them.

- Arrange low shelves and tables in a way that discourages children from running from place to place. If the teacher must constantly remind the children not to run in the classroom, it might very well be sign that too many "runways" are available.

- Arrange furniture so that all children can be seen, from all areas of the classroom. The teacher should be able to scan the classroom easily, in order to locate every child. Adequate supervision is a must at all times.

- Divide the classroom into interest areas for specific types of activities. Such interest areas may include the following: dramatic play area, block area, table toy or manipulative area, art area, listening station, water and sand table, book corner, writing center, music area, and computer center. This helps children become organized in their thoughts, work, and play.

- Label all shelves with pictures and words. This will enable the children to clean up their materials with ease, and they will begin to make the association between the written word and the spoken word. Provide pictures that are large enough for young children to recognize. Tracing different play materials is another option, as long as the outline of the materials is easy to recognize. For example, you can trace a few unifix cubes, color the cubes, print the words, "unifix cubes," beneath the picture, and then place the label on the shelf. In addition to the label on the shelf, you should also place a matching label on the container that holds the unifix cubes. Words can either be printed or typed, and should be large enough for children to point to each letter. Font 48, for example, enables children to do this. Try to use font 48 or larger whenever possible.

Suggestions for Designing Each Interest Area

Dramatic Play Area:

- The following items should be available to help children develop optimal play experiences: child-sized house furniture, such as table and chairs, kitchen appliances, cabinets for storing dishes, rocking chair, and chest of drawers; plastic or some type of unbreakable dishes, cups, utensils, pots and pans; dolls (which depict a variety of different cultures) baby bottles; dress-up clothes for boys and girls; and props and accessories such as purses, briefcases, telephones, wallets, writing pads and pencils and pens, books and magazines. Theme-related materials may also be provided. For example, during the thematic unit, "Pets," providing cat or dog dishes and toy animals will give children the chance to act out and practice the information they have been learning. They could pretend to feed the pets, take them to the vet, or just take them for a walk!

- Open-ended materials can be used for "pretend food." Provide real cereal boxes and other types of empty, real food containers. Allow children to use unifix cubes, large pegs, or clean bottle tops (plastic milk bottle tops work well) for food. In doing so, children are developing their imaginations and their ability to use one object to represent another. This is an important pre-reading skill.

- Provide materials for both boys and girls, and which will accommodate different developmental, social, and cultural needs.

Block Area:

- Low shelves that have pictures and word labels for different blocks work well for teaching children how to organize and sort.

- At least three different building materials should be available each day. For example, duplo blocks, wooden unit blocks, and soft blocks represent three different types of building materials.

- Props, such as people or animal figurines, and transportation vehicles should be provided. Consider the thematic unit of study when adding props to the block area. For example, if the class is learning about the "ocean," an assortment of small, toy sea creatures will entice children to build underwater scenes, or large and small boats!

Table Toys or Manipulatives:

- Label all shelves with words and pictures to help children with their clean-up efforts.
- Place toys and manipulatives in clear, plastic containers with no lids, which allow children to see the contents. When tops are left on containers, children cannot easily see their choices and often such toys are left untouched.
- Give this area a "name" that makes sense to the children. If it is named, "the manipulative area," the children will not only have a difficult time saying the word "manipulative," they will also be confused about its contents. "Manipulative" is not a word that most young children hear often, and, therefore, they cannot relate it to specific types of toys or materials. Suggested names include: "Table Toys," "Toys and Games," "Quiet Area."
- Provide open-ended toys, which may be used in a variety of different ways to help strengthen the imaginations and symbolic thought processes of children. Examples of open-ended materials include: duplos, unifix cubes, large pegs and pegboards, nesting cups, counters, and inch cubes.

Art Area:

- Label shelves with pictures and words, to assist children's clean-up efforts.
- Provide an assortment of paper. Include colored paper, white drawing paper, manila paper, and at least three different sizes of paper—small, medium, and large.
- Give children the choice of using glue bottles or glue sticks, if possible.
- Safety scissors should be available, after the class has learned about the scissor "safety rules." (Discuss the proper way to hold scissors while walking, and the things that may be cut.)
- "Found" materials are a must for a properly stocked art area. Include some of the following materials: cardboard tubes, plastic milk-bottle tops, twist-ties, cotton balls, small boxes, empty spools, plastic spoons, old greeting cards, and magazines. Three-dimensional materials allow children to create all types of wonderful art. Be sure to ask them to describe their work!
- Other art materials that should be consistently available to the children, after they have learned the correct ways to use them, include: scotch tape, pipe-cleaners, paint and paintbrushes, markers and crayons, pencils, and staplers.

Daily Routine

Young children learn best through the use of a consistent daily routine that provides a balance of active and quiet activities throughout the day. When children know what to expect and can predict what is coming next, they learn to organize their thoughts and are less inclined to misbehave. Providing a balance between active and quiet activities also will eliminate much misbehavior, which is often caused by too many quiet activities that are back to back.

To help children learn the daily routine, provide picture cards labeled with words so children can see the order of their day. Place these cards in a prominent place, in the correct sequence. For example, placing the cards below the front board in the classroom would ensure that they were seen by all children during circle time. If a child gets up during morning circle time and wanders to the housekeeping area, guide him/her back to the circle while pointing to the daily routine cards. Show the child where circle time is at the start of the day, and then show him/her when center time will come. Often, just knowing that there will be a time during the day that he/she will be able to play is enough to stop any further misbehavior.

See the following pages for examples of a half-day schedule and a full-day schedule. Note the alternating active and quiet activities.

Half-Day Routine:

8:30 a.m. — 8:45 a.m.: **Greeting Circle** (includes greeting song, calendar activities, brief "character education" discussion, and 1 music and movement activity)

8:45 a.m. — 9:15 a.m.: **Language and Literacy Activity** (includes a discussion about the theme of study, usually in the form of a story web or chart, followed by the thematic story and then story extension activity)

9:15 a.m. — 9:30 a.m.: **Music and Movement Activity** (includes creative movement activities, and the opportunity for children to use musical instruments, rhythm sticks, scarves, and other props while singing and dancing)

9:30 a.m. — 9:50 a.m.: **Small Group Activity** (includes a math or science activity for the children to explore and manipulate, while the class is divided in half with an adult facilitating each small group)

9:50 a.m. — 10:20 a.m.: **Outdoor Game/Playground** (includes a group game and the opportunity for children to use playground equipment such as climbing apparatus, riding toys, digging in sandbox, kicking and throwing balls, and swings)

10:20 a.m. — 10:30 a.m.: **Snack Time**

10:30 a.m. — 11:15 a.m.: **Center Time** (includes a brief "planning period" in which children decide where they plan to work, the actual "work time" in the chosen centers, and then a brief "review" of activities)

11:15 a.m. — 11:30 a.m.: **Closing Circle** (includes a recap of the day, discussing favorite activities, story, and/or other important aspects of the day, along with a "good-bye" song)

Full-Day Routine
(Please see the "Half-Day Routine" for explanation of certain components of the day.)

8:00 a.m. — 8:30 a.m.: **Breakfast**

8:30 a.m. — 8:50 a.m.: **Greeting Circle**

8:50 a.m. — 9:20 a.m.: **Language and Literacy Activity**

9:20 a.m. — 9:40 a.m.: **Music and Movement Activity**

9:40 a.m. — 10:00 a.m.: **Small Group Activity**

10:00 a.m. — 10:30 a.m.: **Outdoor Game**

10:30 a.m. — 11:45 a.m.: **Center Time**

11:45 a.m. — 12:15 p.m.: **Lunch Time**

12:15 p.m. — 12:30 p.m.: **Story**

12:30 p.m. — 12:45 p.m.: **Prepare for rest** (includes bathroom break for all children, placement of cots or mats, and playing soft "background" music)

12:45 p.m. — 1:45 p.m.: ***Rest Time**

1:45 p.m. — 2:00 p.m.: **Snack Time**

2:00 p.m. — 2:30 p.m.: **Playground Time**

2:30 p.m. — 2:50 p.m.: **Closing Circle**

*As children age the need for an hour rest time may diminish. However, some students in the class will still require that period of rest. For those who are outgrowing the nap, inform the child that for the first 10-15 minutes each child must remain on the cot/mat. This will allow time for those that need rest to fall asleep. Try providing books for the non-nappers. Perhaps you could allow the child to work quietly on the computer or other quiet, table activity, while the others rest. Remind the child of the "rest time rules." For example, "work quietly without disturbing others."

**If children stay later than 3:00 p.m., add another Center Time, giving them the chance for more choices of play experiences.

Adult-Child Interaction

The latest brain research supports the idea that children learn best in child-centered classrooms where they are allowed to explore and create, with the guidance and support of caring adults. When early childhood teachers allow children to become actively involved in classroom activities, the children develop an increased level of confidence in their cognitive abilities. They develop a "can do" attitude as they learn to share ideas, explore new materials, and converse with other students and teachers.

Classroom behaviors are managed more easily through the use of encouragement strategies. As teachers encourage young children, a strong emotional bond is created between students and teacher. Once this bond is formed, students often comply with classroom rules because they feel secure within the classroom setting. Examples of encouragement strategies include the following: getting down on the child's physical level to talk; describing the child's work; and joining in the child's play, allowing the child to be the leader. If used consistently and sincerely, encouragement will help keep classroom management problems to a minimum.

See the next pages for a few examples of how to use encouragement strategies throughout different parts of the daily routine.

Circle Time: To encourage children to come to the circle and sit, position yourself at the circle area, and begin singing the names of those children who are sitting quietly (to the tune of "Are You Sleeping?"). Continue singing, adding the names of children who have come to the circle.

Sing, *"Emily is ready, Frank is ready,*
to begin, to begin.
Jessica is ready, Toby is ready,
So is Mark, and Shaun is too!"

It is almost certain that you will soon be singing every child's name in the class. They are encouraged to come to the circle to hear you sing their names. Once all have arrived at the circle and you sing their names, congratulate everyone for a job well done and quickly move on to your circle activities.

Small Group Activity Time: Bring yourself down to the physical level of the child and say, "Sammy, can you tell me about your work?" If Sammy does not reply, describe what you see. "You used lots of blue on the top of the paper and some purple on the sides, and I see yellow circles all over." This type of encouraging comment lets him know that you are really aware of what he has made, and it helps him feel proud about his accomplishment. Another strategy would be to sit down near Sammy and paint the same thing he has painted. Again, he will feel proud that you like his work enough to make the same thing for yourself.

Center Time: Observe and listen carefully as the children work and play, and then enter their play, being certain not to take over or change their play. Mimic the actions of the children, and soon you will be invited to join in. Take directions from the child and ask open-ended questions to extend the child's thinking. For example, if the child directs you to "take the baby to the doctor," ask that child, "why does the baby need to see the doctor?" Becoming a player in the children's activities is an encouragement strategy. It is also the perfect opportunity to build language skills and help children learn to problem-solve. Children will often remain at one activity for longer periods if there is a caring adult involved.

Music/Movement Activities: Don't be just the "director," be a participant as well! As you march and move with the class, those children who are a bit more timid, or who might be afraid, will feel encouraged by your actions. They are sure to join in on your fun!

Additional positive guidance strategies to help with classroom management include the following:

- Redirection: By drawing the attention of the troubled child to a different activity, object, or topic, the teacher can "distract" the child into compliance. For example, if, during circle time, the children become disruptive by talking or shouting while you are trying to talk, turn to your music cabinet, peek inside, and say, "Would you like to come out and meet the children?" (Be sure to place a stuffed animal or puppet inside your cabinet beforehand.) Pretend you are talking to the animal, without showing it to the children. Say, "Oh, you're afraid to come out? What if I ask the boys and girls to be very quiet, will you come out and meet them?" Then, whisper to the children, asking them to stay nice and quiet so your friend can come out to visit. Bring the puppet out of the cabinet, introduce it to all, and then continue with your lesson.

- <u>Natural consequences:</u> Teaching children about what will occur naturally if they continue with a certain undesirable behavior will often stop the behavior. An example would include the following: "If you pour too much glue on your paper, you will not be able to take it home today because the glue will not be dry." Let's say the child did not heed your warning and poured too much glue. When it is time to pack up to go home, show the child how wet the glue is. The picture will have to remain in school until the glue has dried.

- <u>Positive Reinforcement:</u> Giving attention for positive actions is so powerful when trying to extinguish negative behaviors. Try to ignore misbehaviors if they are not harmful to the child or others. Instead, comment on the positive action, as soon as it occurs. If, for example, the child refuses to sit at the circle during circle time, and instead moves away without harming anyone, ignore that behavior. Give lots of attention to the boys and girls at the circle who are following the rules. When bringing out the rhythm sticks and noticing that the child has moved into the circle, give him/her a pair of sticks and let him know how good it is that he/she has joined the class! Soon, that child will always want to remain with the class, for that is where the attention is received.

Literacy Activities

Where the Butterflies Grow

- Read *Where the Butterflies Grow* by Joanne Ryder

- Discussion questions: "How is this story different from *The Very Hungry Caterpillar?*" Display both books. "Which book is about a real caterpillar and which is about a pretend caterpillar? How do you know?" Create the following web:

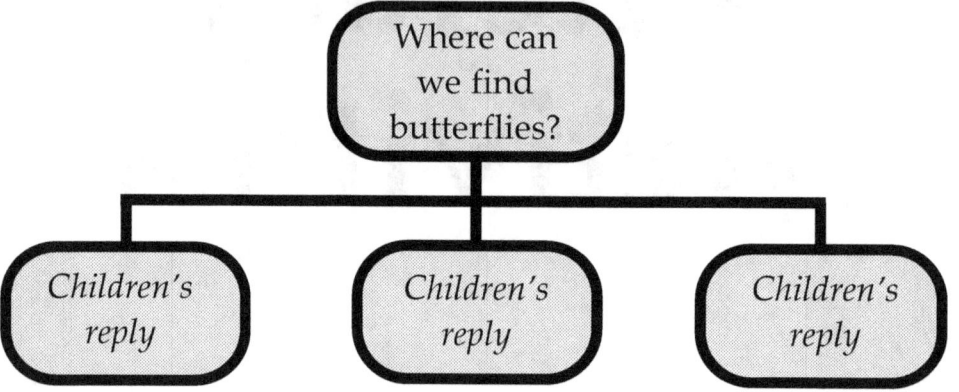

- Follow-up activity: Creep and crawl like a caterpillar. Begin the activity by asking all children to wiggle one of their forefingers like a caterpillar crawling across the floor. Have them "crawl" the caterpillars onto their legs, then their stomachs, then necks, and all the way up to their heads. Ask all children to kneel and move as if they were a new baby caterpillar just hatching from its egg. Have children move like a hungry caterpillar in search of food. Children can spin their chrysalises and pretend to sleep, as they grow wings and change into butterflies. Ask children to demonstrate how they would break out of their chrysalises and fly in search of flowers to eat and drink.

Suggested Themes: Insects, Spring, Butterflies and Caterpillars

Thought of the day...
"A teacher is one who brings us tools and enables us to use them."
—Jean Toomer

Teacher Tips

Have these two books available: *The Very Hungry Caterpillar* and *Where the Butterflies Grow*. In order for the children to thoroughly understand the discussion questions, be sure to have read *The Very Hungry Caterpillar* prior to implementing the activity.

I'm Going to be a Police Officer

- Display the book *I'm Going to be a Police Officer* by Edith Kunhardt.

- Vocabulary Building: Write the question, "How does a police officer help us?" inside the word web and ask children to tell you different ways the police officer helps us.

- While reading the story point out other "helpers" (ex. ambulance driver). Discuss different ways in which police officers help us. Ask if anyone knows about the numbers 9-1-1. Discuss how that number can be used to reach the police, if needed. Discuss what an emergency is. Provide examples of emergencies and non-emergencies and ask children to identify whether the situation is an emergency or non-emergency.

- Follow-up Activity: Cut out the numbers 9-1-1, using sand paper. Tape the numbers to a table and have the children use crayon rubbings to create "9-1-1."

Suggested Themes: Community Helpers, Police Officers

Thought of the day...
"I hear and I forget. I see and I remember. I do and I understand"
—Chinese Proverb

Teacher Tips

When creating a web with four-year-old children it is not necessary to record every child's response. Rather, record only 3-4 responses to each question. Be sure to keep the responses brief to alleviate a long wait time.

Alphabears

For use with the book *Alphabears* (an ABC book) by Kathleen Hague.

- Read and discuss story.

- Provide an assortment of large letters (8 inch size). Each child will choose 1 letter.

- Children decorate their letters, turning them into "alphapets."

- Help children name their pets with a name that begins with the letter, if possible. For example, the alphapet "N" might be named "Noodle!"

Suggested Themes: Pets, Family, and Feelings

Thought of the day...
"Anyone who stops learning is old, whether twenty or eighty."
—Henry Ford

Teacher Tips

Display the story and ask children to describe the picture. Explain that some people do not have real pets but like to pretend with toys or stuffed animals. Ask the children to share what type of pet they have or would like to have.

The Bear's Toothache

For use with the book *The Bear's Toothache* by David McPhail.

Get It Together

- White egg shells or a whole egg (Children will not touch. This is for a demonstration.)
- ¼ cup of cola or tea.
- Raffi's Singable Songs—"Brushing Teeth Song."
- Toothbrush and toothpaste.

Let's Get Started

- After reading the story discuss other things the bear could have done for his toothache. Ask, "why do you think his tooth became sore?"

- Discuss the importance of brushing our teeth.

- Display white eggshells of the egg, explaining that the shells are made of the same material from which our teeth are made (calcium).

- Place shells in cola and leave for at least an hour.

- Sing and act out Raffi's "Brushing Teeth Song."

- Check egg shells later in the day. Show children how foods can stain our teeth.

- If available, brush shell with toothpaste to show how clean it can become.

Suggested Themes: Dental Health, The Dentist, My Healthy Body, Nutrition or Healthy Foods

Thought of the Day…
"The purpose of education is to awaken joy in creative expression and knowledge."

Teacher Tips

After reading the story the activity is designed to be a demonstration. It will take at least an hour for the eggshell to change colors. Move on to other activities and come back to it at a later time of day.

Chrysanthemum

Use with the book *Chrysanthemum* by Kevin Henkes.

- Read the story and discuss.

- After reading the story ask the following questions: "Who was being respectful to Chrysanthemum?" Find parts of the story to support each answer.

- Turn to the playground picture of a child hanging on the bars. Ask the question, "Is this a safe action? Why or why not?"

- Print your name on the board (ex. Miss Jones).

- Demonstrate how to count the letters in your name. Ask each child to count the letter in his or her name.

- Compare answers; "Who has the most letters? Who has the least letters? Who has the same amount of letters?"

Suggested Themes: All About Me, Alike and Different

Thought of the Day:
"Building boys and girls is better than mending men and women."
— *Anonymous*

Sue	Ryan	Alex	Joshua
"least" number of letters	"same" number of letters	"same" number of letters	"most" number of letters

Teacher Tips

It is important to have each child's name printed on a sentence strip or long piece of paper prior to beginning the activity. This will help to avoid a long wait time and to keep the activity interesting.

Humpty Dumpty

- Recite and act out "Humpty Dumpty," using flannel board pieces. Ask the following questions: "Was it safe for Humpty Dumpty to sit on such a high wall? Why did he fall? Why couldn't the men put him back together? If you saw a friend fall off a wall, who would you call for help? Do you think a doctor could help Humpty Dumpty?"

- Bring out two eggs, explaining that 1 egg was cooked and 1 was not. Let children compare the eggs.

- Make a brick wall (out of cardboard block or other available materials).

- Have children make predictions about what will happen to each egg.

- Chorally recite "Humpty Dumpty" as you let the eggs fall (do not do this on carpeting, as the uncooked eggs will break).

- Discuss the differences

Suggested Themes: Community Helpers, Same and Different

Thought of the day:
It's better to try and fail than to fail to try"

—*Anonymous*

Teacher Tips

Gather flannel board pieces of Humpty Dumpty prior to beginning the lesson. If commercially made flannel pieces are not available construct the following pieces: a wall, Humpty Dumpty, horses with men on them, and a broken egg. A piece of Velcro or flannel, glued to the back of the object will adhere to a flannel board. Allow children to work with these flannel pieces during center time activities to enhance the literacy experience.

If You Give a Mouse a Cookie

Use with the book *If You Give A Mouse A Cookie* by Laura Joffe Numeroff.

- Display the story and ask, "What type of pet do you see?" What do you think he is doing?

- Take a picture-walk through the book and ask, "Do you think this is a real or pretend story? Why?"

- Read title, author, and story. Discuss.

- Ask each child to imagine a pet he/she would like to have.

- Tell the children that something usually happens when you give a pet some "people food."

- Let them fill in the following blanks: "If you give a _____ a _____, he'll want a _____ to go with it."

- Ask each child to draw a picture of the sentence.

- Put all pictures in a class book. A suggested title for the book could be, "If You Give A Pet Some People Food...."

Suggested Themes: Family, Pets

"If you give an <u>alligator</u> a <u>cookie</u>, he'll want a <u>fish</u> to go with it."

Thought of the day...
"Learning is a treasure that will follow its owner everywhere."
—Chinese Proverb

Teacher Tips

When taking a "picture-walk" through a book, display the pictures but do not read the words. Ask the children to share their ideas about what they see in the pictures. The picture-walk will help to build background knowledge and give a purpose for reading the book.

I Want to be an Astronaut

Read *I Want To Be An Astronaut* by Byron Barton

- Display the book and ask about the picture on the cover.

- Read the title, author, and book.

- Ask, "How is the space shuttle different from an airplane?" Discuss their responses.

Record responses on chart as follows:

Airplane	Space Shuttle
1.	1.
2.	2.
3.	3.

Follow up:

- As an artistic exercise, ask children what might be living in outer space (friendly or mean, big or small, etc.) What types of bodies could they have?

- Children design and create "creatures from outer space" from a variety of art materials (cotton balls, pipe cleaners, craft sticks, buttons, glitter, etc.).

Suggested Themes: Space, Air Transportation, Jobs People Do

Thought for the day:
We can do anything we want to do if we stick to it long enough.
—Helen Keller

Teacher Tips

Be sure to provide clear pictures of an airplane and space shuttle before implementing this activity. Because abstract thought has not been fully developed at this age, providing visual clues is necessary for the children to fully understand this activity.

Pet Show

For use with the book *Pet Show* by Ezra Jack Keats.

- Display the story and ask children to describe the picture. Take a brief picture-walk and then find the picture of the boy with the jar.

- Ask, "What do you think could be in the jar?"

- Read the title, author, and story to find out.

- After the story and discussion, have the children line up their pets ("toy pets" which they brought from home) so all can see them.

- Sort them in a variety of ways (big, small, medium, by color, by the number of legs, fluffy/not fluffy, etc.).

- Present each pet with a blue ribbon (teacher created) for various categories such as, "quietest dog," "bluest bird," "fastest snake," etc. Use the story as a guide for titles on ribbons.

Suggested Themes: Pets, Community Helpers, Family, Germs

Thought of the day...
"When you're through changing, you're through."

—*Anonymous*

Teacher Tips

Prior to reading the story send home a note asking parents' permission for each child to bring in a *toy* pet. The toy may be a stuffed animal or plastic toy. You may want to use the example of the note found on the following page. Be sure to provide extra stuffed animals or toys for those children who do not bring in their own.

Dear Families,

Our class has been learning about different types of "pets." We would like to have a class "Pet Show," so the children can count, pattern, sort, and measure the different animals.

Please allow your child to bring in 1 toy animal for our pet show, on _____.

It can be a stuffed animal or a plastic or rubber toy, and may be any type of animal. (Please do not send in anything breakable or of great value.)

Thank you for your help with this fun math activity!

Trucks

Read *Trucks* by Donald Crews.

- Display the book *Trucks* by Donald Crews. Ask if anyone can figure out the name of the story.

- Show the 2 pictures that display a highway with many cars and trucks.

- Ask them to explain what they see.

- Create the following "web" and ask the children for their ideas:

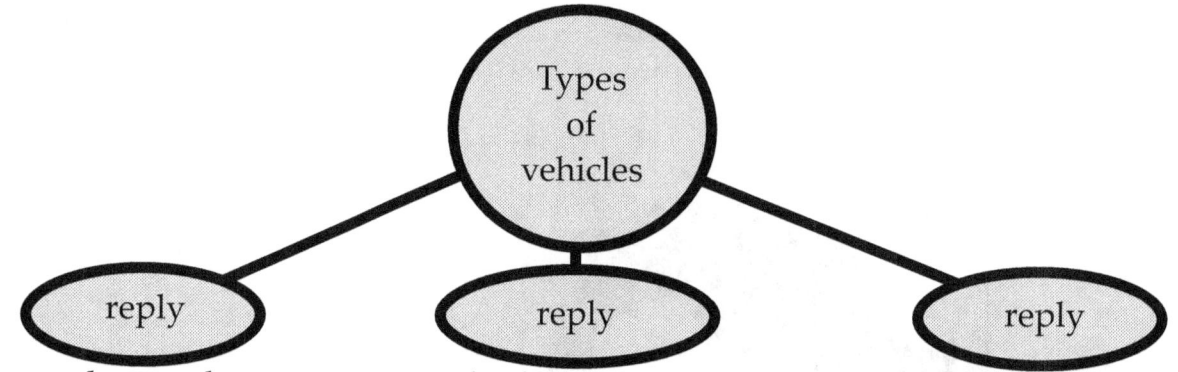

- Point to the word as you say it and ask if they know what a vehicle is (means of transporting with wheels).

- Ask, "What kinds of vehicles do you see in this picture? What are some other types of vehicles?"

- Read the wordless book.

- Record the different names of vehicles on a mural paper. Children draw representations of each type of vehicle next to the appropriate name.

Suggested Themes: Transportation, Community Helpers, Jobs People Do

Thought of the day…
"Education…is a painful, continual, and difficult work to be done in kindness, by watching, by warning…by praise, but above all, by example.
—John Ruskin

Teacher Tips

This book contains no words, only pictures. When reading a wordless book, let the children know that these books are equally important as books with words. Although they contain no words, the pictures can still tell a story.

Harry the Dirty Dog Story Mural

Get It Together

- Large piece of mural paper divided into four sections/columns: First, Next, Then, Last.

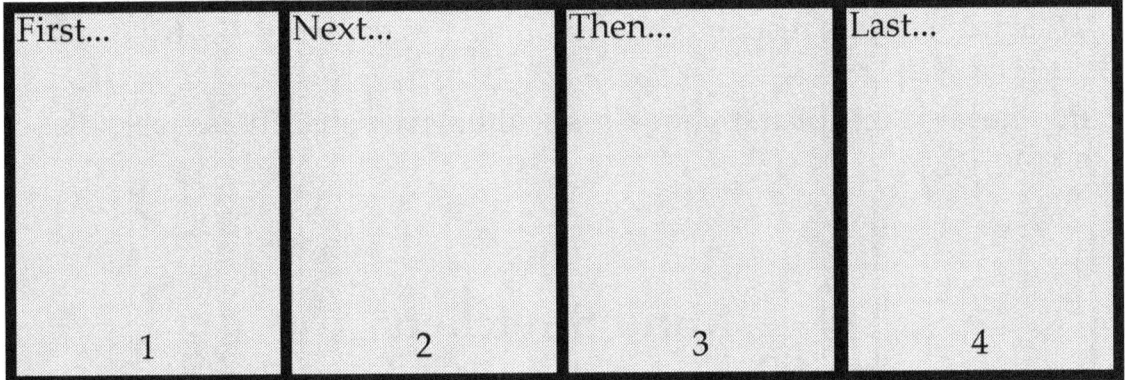

- Pictures of Harry the Dog: Harry as a clean dog, Harry in the bathtub, Harry resting on a pillow. See the following pages for pictures.

- Craft sticks, tissue paper, paper towel tubes, sand, and/or various other art supplies.

Let's Get Started

- Read the story *Harry the Dirty Dog* by Gene Zion prior to this activity.

- In section 1 of the chart, place a picture of clean Harry and ask the children to explain what happened first. Record their explanations (1 or 2 sentences) on the mural, after the word "first."

- In section 2, have the children design pictures of the different ways that Harry got dirty. Example: provide cardboard tubes and see if anyone creates the "tunnel" through which Harry crawled. Provide a variety of art materials so children can create a 3-dimensional scene (ex: craft sticks, tissue paper to crumble, brown rice or sand to use for dirt—painted with tempera paint). Let children tell you about their pictures and encourage them to "write" words. Rewrite their words describing how Harry got dirty.

- In section 3 place a picture of Harry in the bathtub. Ask children to describe what happened. Record their explanations (1 or 2 sentences). Print their explanation next to the word "then" in section 3. Ask, "How did Harry get clean?" Record those responses on the mural next to the bathtub (ex. bath, soap, water, brush, family, towel, etc.).

- In section 4 place a picture of Harry, nice and clean and relaxing on the pillow. Ask the children to describe Harry at the end of the book. "How do you think Harry feels?" Record the class response on mural, next to the word "last."

- When the mural is completed your class will have created the sequence of events in *Harry the Dirty Dog*.

Mind Stretchers

- For the developmentally young learner, discuss the ways Harry got clean. Record those responses next to a picture of Harry in the bathtub.

- For the more advanced learner, discuss ways in which children get dirty (ex: playing in the dirt, fingerpainting, etc.). Record the responses on a large piece of paper. Ask the students to illustrate each response.

Teacher Tips

When creating a mural with children divide your class in half and work with a maximum of 9 children per mural. It would be better to make additional murals rather than include more than 9 students at a mural.

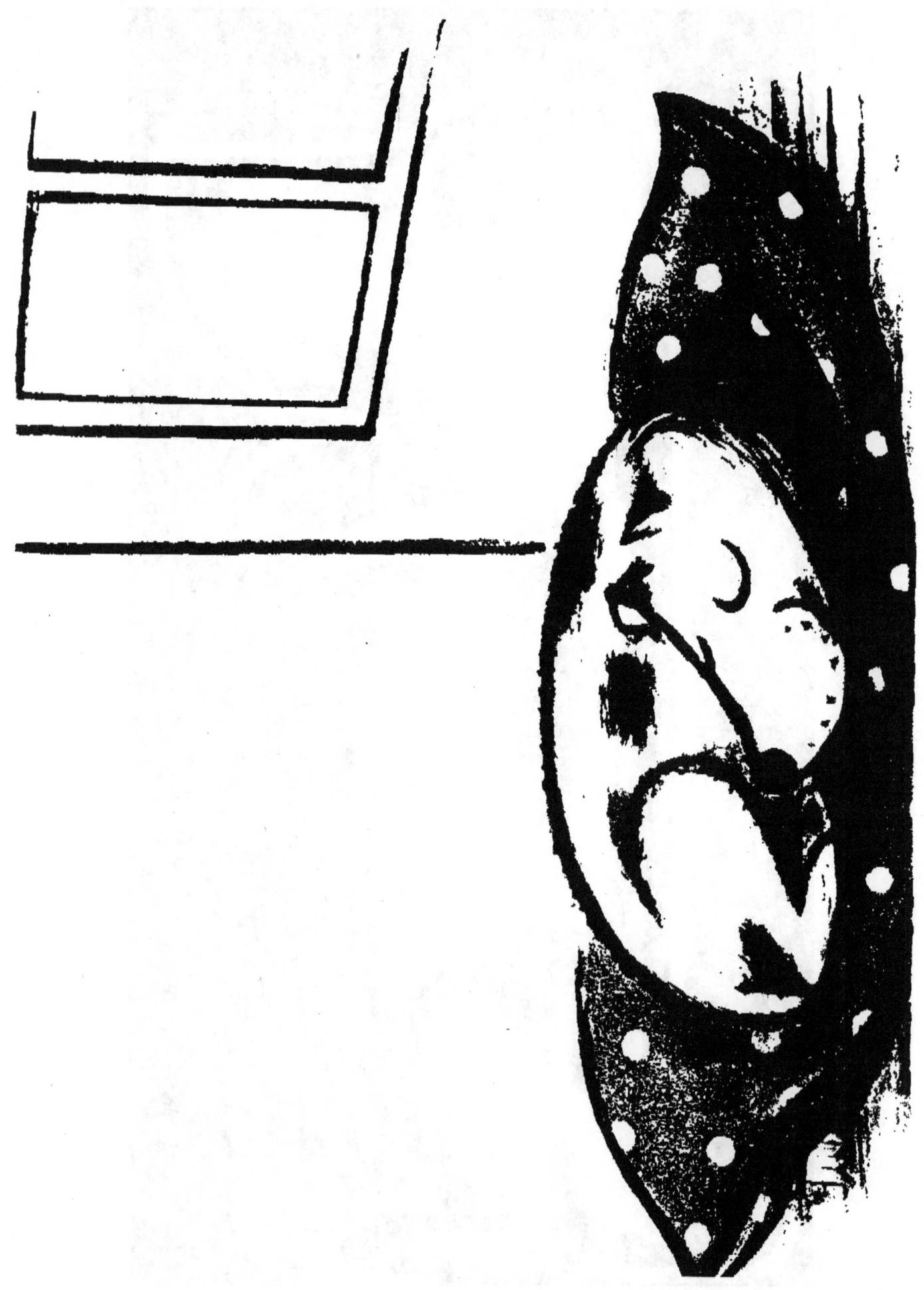

The Snowman

Read *The Snowman* by Raymond Briggs.

- Display the book, reading title and author.

- Take a picture-walk through the book.

- Ask if anyone notices something different about this book (it is a wordless book). Explain that sometimes you can "read" the pictures to tell a story.

- Encourage the children to become involved in the story.

- Ask, "Do you think the snowman could live in a warm state like Florida? Why? Why not? Could the snowman live in our town? Why, why not?

- Have the children make a class snowman. Crumble and stuff newspaper into 2 white bags, then have the children decorate the face and decorate the body. Use the book as a guide.

Suggested Themes: Winter & Ice-Skating

Thought of the day…
"Write on your heart that every day is the best day of the year"
—*Ralph Waldo Emerson*

Teacher Tips

Introduce this activity in a large group setting. Then divide the children into two or more smaller groups (depending upon your class size) so that all children may participate in this activity. Each group should have the following materials: two white plastic trash bags, materials for decorating the snowman, and enough newspaper to stuff each bag. Children should crumple the paper and stuff the bags to strengthen hand and finger muscles.

Ira Sleeps Over

Read *Ira Sleeps Over* by Bernard Waber.

- Prepare a Venn diagram (shown below) on chart or mural paper.

- Display the story and discuss the cover.

- Take a picture picture-walk through the book.

- Discuss the different facial expressions on the boy.

- Ask, "What do you think is happening? Why is it sometimes difficult to play with friends at night?"

- Read title, author and story to find out.

- Children look through magazines and cut out pictures of day and night.

- Some pictures will represent things that are used during day *and* at night, so discuss how they can be placed between the two groups, using a Venn diagram.

The middle of a Venn diagram shares the same characteristics as both circles.

Suggested Themes: Camping, Friends, Teddy Bears

Thought of the day…
"He who has imagination without learning has wings but no feet."
—Joseph Joubert

Teacher Tips

A Venn diagram is designed to demonstrate similarities and differences between two groups. The intersection of the two circles is the place to write similarities between the two groups. For young children, it is helpful to make each circle a different color. For example, one circle could be red and one could be blue. Use a blue marker for things that are seen only in the blue area. Use a red marker for those things seen only in the red area. Use both red and blue in the intersection of the diagram.

The Little Red Hen

Read *The Little Red Hen* by Lucinda McQueen.

- Display the cover of *The Little Red Hen* and ask the children to describe what they see.

- Read to find out why some animals are resting while the hen is working.

- Ask, "How did the hen feel when her friends would not help?"

- How would you feel if you were the only one cleaning up after your friends played with your toys?

- After reading story have children role play the animals, but instead have all the animals help make the bread. Share a loaf of warm (micro-waved) bread, if available. (Micro-waveable bread can be found in most grocery stores in the dairy case.)

Follow-up Activity:

   Materials:
   - White bread one or two slice(s) per child.
   - White school glue (not a glue stick).
   - Liquid soap (dish or hand soap).
   - Liquid tempera paint.

- Have children remove the crust on the bread. (They can feed it to the birds during "outside time.")

- Pour one tablespoon of white glue on each slice of bread.

- Children knead and squeeze glue and bread together until it turns into a ball.

- Add a few drops of liquid soap to the bread and glue mixture and squeeze throughout the dough. The soap will keep the dough from becoming sticky.

- Ask children to make their favorite farm animals; model as with any clay.

- Allow the animal sculptures to dry completely and then paint.

Mind Stretchers

- For the developmentally young learner sing "Old MacDonald Had A Farm" as the animals are placed on display.

- For the more advanced learner allow the child to use creative spelling to make labels to place in front of animals.

Suggested themes: Farm, Healthy Foods, Zoo

Thought of the day…
"We make a living by what we get, but we make a life by what we give."
—Winston Churchill

Teacher Tips

Provide a pre-made example of a simple farm animal. Tell the students that you created this animal from a special kind of dough that they are going to create together. Ask students to guess what material you used to make your animal.

A Letter to Amy

Book: *A Letter to Amy* by Ezra Jack Keats.

- Display story and discuss the cover.

- Take a picture-walk through the book, and ask, "What do you think the boy is doing?" (Point out pictures that may be familiar: chalk drawing on sidewalk, hopscotch board, lightening in the sky, mailbox birthday hats, etc.)

- Read title, author, and story to find out what is happening. Then give the child a paper that has the heading of a letter, "Dear _____."

- Tell the child that they will be "writing" a letter to a friend or family member and that letters start out with the word "Dear." Offer as much or as little assistance as each child needs to complete his or her letter.

- Accept any form of writing, including scribbling, beginning letter formation, etc.

Suggested Themes: Celebrations, Friends, Letters, Invitations

Thought of the day…
"They can because they believe they can."

—*Virgil*

Teacher Tips

Accept any form of scribbling or attempted letter formation as writing. Do not require a child to copy your words. Rather, ask the child what he or she wrote, then ask if he or she would like for you to rewrite the words beneath his or her writing.

Gone Fishing

Read *Gone Fishing* by Earlene Long.

- Display story and discuss the cover.

- Ask, "Who do you think these people are? What do you think they are doing?"

- Take a brief picture-walk through the book.

- Ask, "What is the man doing? What is the boy doing? Do you think they are near a pond or some other body of water? Is it bigger than a pond? Is it a lake? Could it be the ocean?"

Follow-up Activity:

    Materials:
- Paper fish with numbers 1–5 (see example).
- Paper fish with dots 1-5 (see example).
- Paper clips for each fish.
- Magnets and yarn strings.

- Cut out numbered fish, and fish with dots (handouts).

- Place a paper clip on each fish.

- Make 2 fishing poles using yarn and a magnet.

- Scatter fish inside the story circle face down so numbers and dots are hidden.

- Let 2 children at a time "go fishing."

- When all the children have caught a fish, ask them to pair up. (Those with "dots" find corresponding "numbers," those with "numbers" find corresponding "dots.")

Mind Stretchers

- For the developmentally young learner, make fish with only dots. They will find a classmate that has the corresponding dots (ex. if their fish has one dot, they will find the classmate with the matching fish, with only one dot).

- For the more advanced learner add additional fish from numbers 1 through 10.

Suggested Themes: Aquatic Animals, Camping, Summer Fun, Fishing, Nature, Outdoor Sports, and Wildlife

Thought of the day...
"Kind words may be short and easy to speak, but their echoes are truly endless."
—Mother Teresa

Teacher Tips

There should be an equal number (depending on class size) of fish with numbers and fish with dots. For example if you have 10 students, 5 should have a fish with a number on it and 5 should have a fish with the coordinating number of dots on it. For an odd numbered class, the teacher should have the extra fish.

Have You Seen Bugs?

Read *Have You Seen Bugs?* by Joanne Oppenheim or *Bugs! Bugs! Bugs!* by Nancy Winslow Parker.

- Vocabulary building: Create the following web.

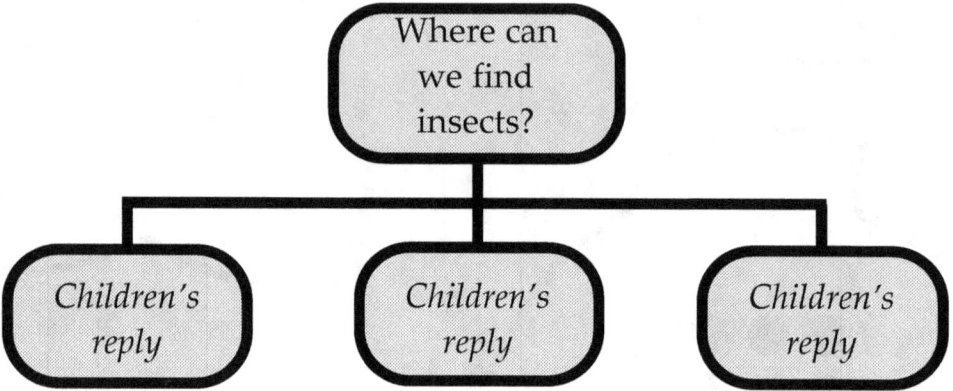

- Discussion questions: Record in the form of a chart. Divide the chart in two: "How can bugs help us? / How can bugs harm us?" Discuss different insects from the story, asking children to describe the different ways bugs can help and harm us. For example, bees help keep our gardens full of flowers by bringing pollen from one flower to another, as they drink the nectar. But they can be harmful with their powerful stingers!

How can bugs help us?	How can bugs harm us?
1.	1.
2.	2.
3.	3.
4.	4.
5.	5.

Follow-up activity: Play "The Very Hungry Spider" game. Children work with partners, taking turns, pretending that their spiders are catching bugs.

- First, each pair is given 1 piece of paper. They can draw a specific amount of spiders across the top of the paper. Provide the matching number of unifix cubes as spiders. (You can coordinate the number of spiders to the "number" that the children are learning that particular day or week.) For example, if the children are working on number 8, they will draw 8 small spiders across the top of the paper. Each pair counts out 8 unifix cubes which are make-believe "bugs!"

- Children place all 8 "bugs" (unifix cubes) at the bottom of the paper.

- One child closes his/her eyes and the other child moves some bugs next to the spiders, and hides the others.

- The child opens his/her eyes and determines how many bugs got away. He/she can do this by placing one bug on top of one spider, and then counting the number of spiders without a "bug."

- Continue playing as long as children are interested.

Suggested Themes: Insects, Spring, Gardens, Dirt, Pond

Thought of the day...
"Children come into the world not knowing who they are.
They learn who they are from those around them."
—Katherine Kersey

Teacher Tips

It is helpful to have a web pre-made and laminated to use over and over. Use a marker that can be erased after each use.

Clifford's Birthday Party

Read *Clifford's Birthday Party* by Norman Bridwell.

- Vocabulary building: Print the following words on cards or sentence strips—decorations, ball, shampoo—and provide examples and discuss uses for each.

- Discussion questions: Take a brief picture-walk through the book before reading and ask, "What is happening? Who are the story characters? What are they doing? Have you ever done any of these things? Do you think this is a real or pretend story? Why?"

Place the following words in a web, and record children's responses:

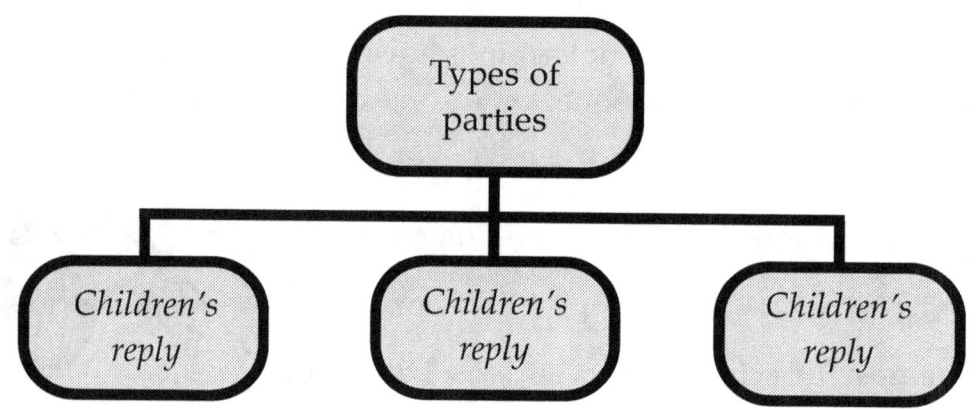

Follow-up activity: Each child will draw a birthday cake for Clifford. Instead of candles, give each child three "dog bones," which have the numerals, 1, 2, 3, along with the correct number of dots on them. After children decorate their cakes, they cut out the dog bones, placing them in order on the birthday cake.

Suggested Themes: Friends, Celebrations, Shapes

Thought of the day…
"No one cares how much you know, until they know how much you care."
—*Don Swartz*

"Bones" for Clifford's cake.

Teacher Tips

Allow children to create their own birthday cakes. It is not necessary to supply a pattern. Rather than being focused on the finished product, it is more important for the children to complete the process. Too often "pattern art" will stifle a young child's creativity. As the children are bringing home their creative projects, you may want to discuss with parents, the importance of "the process" of creating, rather than the finished product.

I Am Me

Get It Together

- Story *I Am Me*, by Karla Kuskin.

- Vocabulary cards, with the following words printed: eye, chin, toe, eyebrow, ear, hair, smile.

- A full-body picture of a child.

- Chart:

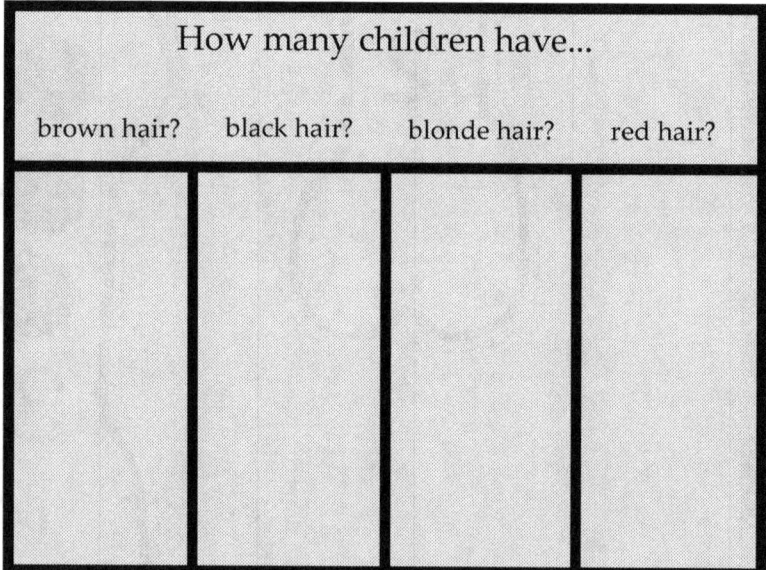

- Print the color words with the matching colors, so children can identify their hair color more easily.

- Markers or crayons that match the hair colors.

Let's Get Started

- Read *I Am Me* by Karla Kuskin.

- Vocabulary building: Have children point to each body part as you read the word: eye, chin, toe, eyebrow, ear, hair, smile. Then place cards (or have a child place cards) on the matching body part of the full-body picture of the child.

- Discussion questions: "In what ways does the little girl in the book look like her mother? Her father? Why does she say that she looks just like herself? Who do you look like?"

Follow-up activity: Display the hair-color graph and ask children to sort themselves by hair color. Each child will then mark the column in which he/she belongs, using markers or crayons that are the same colors as their hair. Count and record the number of marks in each column. Compare amounts. Ask the following questions: "How many children have black hair? Brown hair? Blonde hair? Red hair?" "Do more children in our class have black hair or blonde hair?" "Which hair color has less marks, red or brown?" "Does any color have the same number of marks?"

Suggested Themes: All About Me, Colors, My Healthy Body

Thought of the day:
"Children are like wet cement. Whatever falls on them makes an impression."

Teacher Tips

To avoid a long wait time and to keep the activity interesting, ask two or three students with different colored hair to come up and mark the chart at the same time. Be sure to make the chart large enough for three children to record at the same time.

The Kissing Hand

Read *The Kissing Hand* by Audrey Penn.

- Vocabulary building: Present the word, "friend" in a web, asking children for a few responses to describe a friend.

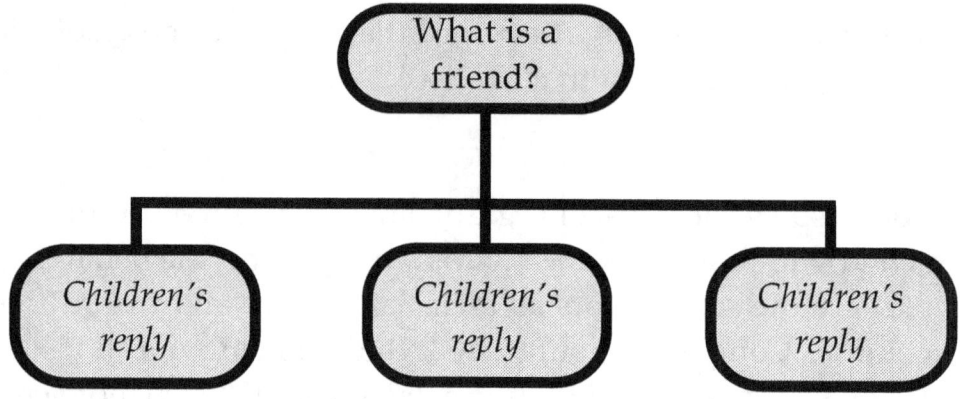

- Discussion questions: Before reading the story, take a brief picture-walk through the book, asking the children, "Who are the story characters? What do you think they are doing? Do you think this is a real or pretend story? Why?"

- After reading, ask the following questions: "When have you been scared? How did you feel, going to school for the first time? What are some things you can do when you miss your mother or other family members?"

Follow-up activity: Before the story is read, tape different colored paper hearts under the students' tables and chairs. Use 4 different colors of paper: pink, red, purple, blue. After reading the story, tell the children you have hidden "kisses" under their tables and chairs. (Explain that "hearts" represent kisses.) When each child has found 2 hearts, he/she gathers back at the circle or story area and sorts the hearts on a color chart, which you have provided. After all children have returned to the story area, count the number of each color heart. Write the number beneath each color. Which color has the most? Least? Same Amount?

Parent/Family Activity: Send a note home to parents, asking them to make a card for their child. Ask them to send the card into school, so you can share it with the class. See the following sample letter on the next page.

Dear Family,

We are reading a book called <u>The Kissing Hand</u>, which is about a raccoon named Chester who is afraid he will miss his mother when he goes to school. His mother gives him a special kiss in the palm of his hand and sends her love with him to school.

We would like your participation with this activity to help your child relate to the story. Please make a "card" for your child with the attached paper. You may want to:

- *Draw a picture.*
- *Write a special note.*
- *Attach a family picture.*
- *Cut out pictures from magazines.*

We will share the cards with the class and then hang them in our Reading Corner. Your child can look at it whenever he or she needs to "connect" with home and remember your love!

Suggested Themes: All About Me, Family, Feelings

Thought of the day…
"If you judge people, you have no time to love them."
— Mother Teresa

Teacher Tips

Before the children arrive, tape different colored paper hearts under the students' chairs. The children should not be able to see the hearts when they enter the classroom, but should be able to find them when they are asked to look for the hidden kisses. Use four different colors for the hearts.

The Grouchy Ladybug

Get It Together

- *The Grouchy Ladybug* by Eric Carle.

- 1 large paper plate (divided in 4 parts, with a center spot- see example), per child.

- Crayons or markers.

- 4 small paper clips per child.

- 1 magnet for each child (magnetic letters or numbers work).

"Ladybug, Ladybug Find Your Way Home"

- After reading *The Grouchy Ladybug*, review the different creatures that the Grouchy Ladybug visited.

- Of those creatures, ask children to choose 4 of their favorites. They will draw one creature in each section of the paper plate.

- The oval in the center of the plate will be the ladybugs' home. The paper clips will represent the ladybugs. Children place their 4 "ladybugs" in the center of the plate.

- Demonstrate how they can use small magnets underneath the plates to move their ladybugs around the plate to visit their friends. Invite them to experiment.

- Make-up a story for the children to follow. Example:
  Once there were 4 ladybugs who lived in the same house. Each one decided to visit a different friend. (Children move 1 paper clip to each section of the plate, using the magnet beneath the plate.) ***Then, the 2 ladybugs at the bottom decided to visit their friends at the top. The 2 on the right side wanted to visit their friends on the left side.*** (Most of the children will probably not be able to differentiate between right and left sides. If they ask, guide them; if they do not, allow them to experiment. It is important for the children to cross the midline, so do not get bogged down with the exact details.) ***Then one ladybug said, "Let's all visit the biggest animal!" All ladybugs moved to the biggest animal on the plate. Another ladybug said, "The smallest friend needs our help. He isn't feeling very well." All ladybugs moved to visit the little sick friend. Suddenly, one ladybug noticed it was getting dark outside, looked at her watch and said, " it's 8:00 o'clock, time for bed! Let's get home!" All ladybugs moved back to the center of the plate and went to sleep.***

- Allow children to work with partners, taking turns, and making up new stories about their ladybugs.

Outdoor Game: "How Many Spots on the Ladybug?"

- Cut out red circles and draw black spots on them. Make matching pairs of "ladybugs" so children can locate their match.

- Hide the "ladybugs" around the playground, or other outdoor area, and allow children to search for 1 ladybug.

- When they have found 1 ladybug, they count the number of spots, and they find a friend with the same number of spots.

- After all children have collected and found their match, place all "ladybugs" spot side up on the ground.

- Children take turns tossing a beanbag onto a ladybug. When the beanbag lands on or near a ladybug, the child picks up the ladybug, counts the number of spots, and finds the ladybug with the matching number of spots. (If there are many children, allow a friend to help search for the match to avoid a long "wait time.")

Suggested Themes: Insects, Spring, Friends, Feelings

Thought of the day…
"Sometimes we have to stop dealing with the misbehavior and heal the relationship first."
—Jane Nelson, Ed.D.

Teacher Tips

Use a maximum of ten dots for each lady bug.

There's an Alligator Under My Bed

Read *There's an Alligator Under My Bed* by Mercer Mayer.

- Vocabulary building: Place the following question in a web and record children's responses.

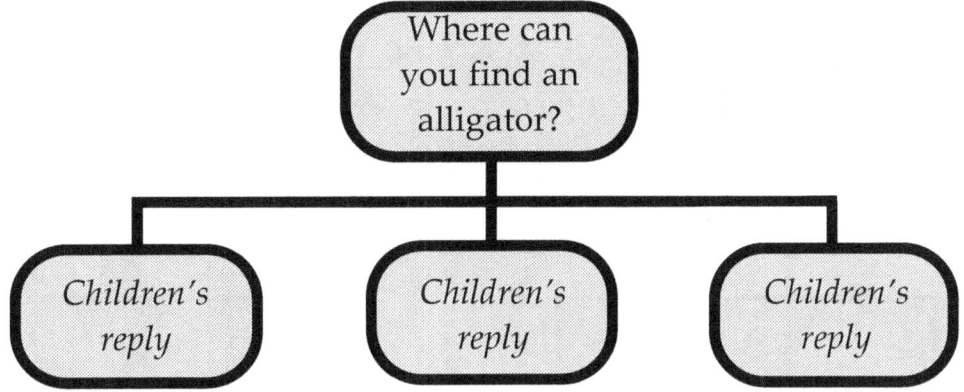

- Discussion questions: "Why did the boy write a note to his father? What are some other reasons why people write notes to other people?"

Follow-up activity: Have each child "write" a note to someone. What types of notes will they write? Will it be a note to "warn" a friend about something, to say "thank you" for a special gift, or just to say "hello?" Praise all attempts at writing. Any attempts at writing should be accepted: scribbling, some letters and shapes, etc.

Suggested Themes: "Writing activities" should be incorporated into every theme of study. Four-year-olds should not be made to copy, but instead, should be encouraged to write the way they can.

Thought of the day...
"What's done to children, they will do to society."
—Dr. Karl Menninger

Teacher Tips

Remember to limit student responses to 3 to 4 responses per question on the web. Some children may not get a chance to participate at this time. If a student really wants to share a response but you've already listed 3 to 4 responses, simply acknowledge the child by saying, "I see you really want to share, but we have no more room to write. The next time you will have a turn." Remember to call on that student the next time.

The Very Hungry Caterpillar

Get It Together

- *The Very Hungry Caterpillar* by Eric Carle.

- 2 sheets of large construction paper, each folded in three sections. (The first sheet of paper will display the following: title of paper; egg; small, thin caterpillar. The second sheet will display the following: a larger, plumper caterpillar; a chrysalis; a butterfly).

For example:

Stages of a Butterfly	3. The hungry caterpillar eats many leaves.
1. A butterfly lays an egg on a leaf.	4. The caterpillar spins a chrysalis around its body.
2. A caterpillar hatches from the egg.	5. A butterfly is born!

- Green paper for making leaves.

- Packing popcorn to represent the "egg." (Each child will only need a small piece of the packing popcorn to represent the egg.)

- Small piece of pipe-cleaner or yarn (approximately 1-2 inches long, per child).

- Glue.

- Safety scissors.

- Hole-punchers.

- 1 cotton ball per child (preferably green or blue).

- Small sticks from a tree (approximately 3 inches long) or craft sticks.

- Masking tape.

- Scotch tape.

- Colorful tissue paper—each child will need 2 squares, approximately 4" x 4" each.

- Pipe-cleaners (approximately 6 inches each).

Let's Get Started

This activity is separated into parts, so children can learn about each stage of the butterfly's development. Guide children through the completion of each part, as you feel they need to progress. Some children may work on the entire project, all at one time, while others will need to work on one part a day until completed.

1. Part 1: Read the story *The Very Hungry Caterpillar* by Eric Carle. Take children for a nature walk around the outside of your school. Provide each child with a magnifying glass, or have partners share. Tell children to look very closely at the leaves using the magnifying glasses to see if they can find any eggs on leaves or flower petals. They can also search for holes in leaves, made by caterpillars. Remind the children to just "look" and not to touch, so that the eggs are not disturbed. (Also, remind children that some insects will sting if they are disturbed.)

2. Part 2: Large paper should be prepared ahead of time, folded in three sections.
    - The "title" will be placed in the top section. You can either have the title pre-printed, or you can have children develop a title, after they complete the activity.

- In the second folded section, children draw and cut out 1 green leaf and glue onto paper. Children cut out a piece of the packing popcorn (to represent the egg) and glue that small piece onto the leaf. Place the pre-printed words beneath the leaf, or have children dictate, as you write their words. (See sample of pre-printed words.)

3. Part 3: Children draw and cut out a green leaf and glue onto the bottom section of the first paper. Then they glue a small, thin caterpillar (one piece of pipe-cleaner or yarn) onto the leaf. Place the pre-printed words beneath the caterpillar and leaf, or have children dictate as you write the words.

4. Part 4: Children draw and cut out a green leaf, and then, pretending to be hungry caterpillars, use hole-punchers to "eat" the leaves. Glue the "chewed" leaf onto the top part of the second piece of paper, which is also folded into three sections. Each child will gently pull and stretch a blue or green cotton ball, to form a large, hungry caterpillar. Discuss how much the caterpillar has grown! Place the pre-printed words beneath the large caterpillark, or have children dictate as you write their words.

5. Part 5: Children wrap small pieces of sticks (or craft sticks) with masking tape. (Tip: Either place a roll of masking tape in a large tape dispenser, or cut several pieces of tape and place along the working table, for easy access. Each child will need at least 3 pieces of tape, 12 inches long.) The wrapped stick will represent the chrysalis. Place the pre-printed words beneath the chrysalis, or have children dictate as you write their words.

6. Part 6: Children choose two pieces of tissue paper (pre-cut squares), grasp them together at the middle, and then wrap a 6 inch piece of pipe-cleaner around the middle, forming a "butterfly." (To make it easier, have children staple the two pieces of tissue paper together at the middle before wrapping the pipe-cleaner.) Children can decorate the butterflies with different colored markers and then glue onto the bottom section. Place the pre-printed words beneath the butterfly, or have children dictate as you write their words.

Sample of pre-printed words:
    Title = "Stages of a Butterfly"
    1. A butterfly lays an egg on a leaf.
    2. A caterpillar hatches from the egg.

3. The hungry caterpillar eats many leaves.
4. The caterpillar spins a chrysalis around its body.
5. A butterfly is born!

Suggested Themes: Insects, Spring, Butterflies and Caterpillars

Thought of the day…
"There will always be some curve balls in your life. Teach children to thrive in that adversity."
—Jeanne Moutoussasamy-Ashe

Teacher Tips

If funding is available you may want to consider purchasing live butterfly larvae and butterfly houses to hatch your own butterflies. This will enable students to see first hand the sequence of development. These larvae are available through various companies and school supply catalogs. A "butterfly release party" could be scheduled and parents could be invited to see the butterflies being released.

Mary Wore Her Red Dress and Henry Wore His Green Sneakers

Read *Mary Wore Her Red Dress and Henry Wore His Green Sneakers* by Merle Peek.

- Vocabulary Building: Print the words, "sneakers," "sweater," and "bandanna" on cards. Read each word as you display the item. Ask children to describe sneakers, sweater, and bandanna and their uses.

- Discussion questions: "Do you think this is a real or pretend story? Why? Have you ever been to a birthday party? What did you wear?"

- Follow-up activity: Sing the song, "Mary Wore Her Red Dress," to the tune of "Did You Ever See a Lassie?" Sing each child's name, describing an article of clothing the child is wearing and its color. As you sing about each child, have the child stand and point to the color about which you are singing. Encourage all children to sing along.

Music and Movement

Play instrumental music, and ask children to move their feet in a "happy" way. Then ask them to move their feet in the following ways: angry, tired, quiet, silly, noisy, as they dance to music. Children may dance with partners, copying their movements. Give each child a colorful scarf to hold and shake, as he/she dances. (Even very shy children will enjoy making the scarf move.)

Suggested Themes: All About Me, Friends, Colors, Feelings

Thought of the day...
"Friendship is the only cement that will ever hold the world together."
—Woodrow Wilson

Teacher Tips

When moving in a creative way, it is helpful for each child to have his or her own space. One idea is to place hula hoops on the floor, with each child moving inside one hoop. You may also ask the students to spread out and be sure that there is adequate space between each child by stretching out their arms, making sure no one is touching.

Here Are My Hands

Read *Here Are My Hands* by Bill Martin Jr. and John Archambault.

• Vocabulary building: Place the words, "what can I do with my hands?" in a web and record children's responses.

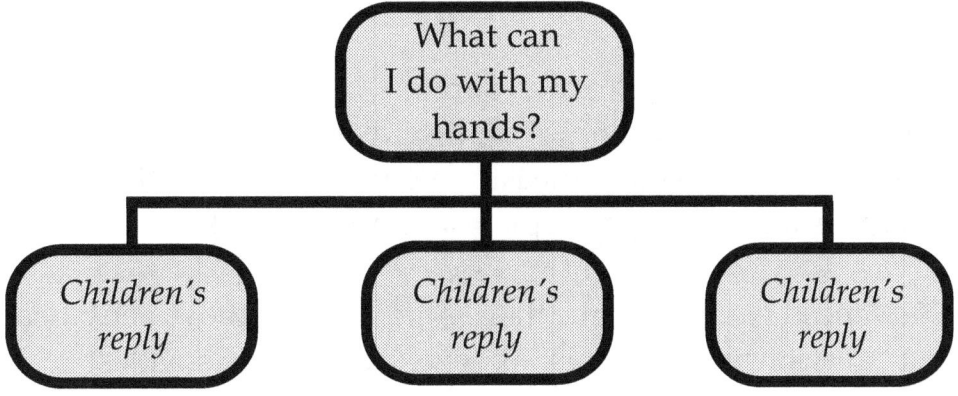

• Have the children demonstrate the following actions: catching and throwing, chewing and brushing.

• Discussion questions: Make a list of different body parts and ask children to describe how each is important. Example:
　　Eyes—for seeing
　　Ears—for hearing and listening
　　Feet—for walking, jumping, running, dancing

Why do we need...

Eyes? _____

Ears? _____

Feet? _____

Follow-up activity: Have children measure classroom items, using their "hands" as the measuring tool. "How many hands long is the book? How many hands long is the cot?" If time permits, children can make several handprints on separate pieces of paper, using large, washable stamp pads or finger paint. They can line up and count the number of hands they used to measure an object.

Mind Stretchers

- For the developmentally young learner, provide manipulatives for measuring classroom items. For example, they can use unifix cubes to measure their feet. Ask, "how many unifix cubes did you need to measure your foot?" Use other manipulatives, as well, such as large, stackable pegs, duplos, and bristle blocks.

- For the more advanced students, have them complete the above activity and then have them put their "measuring materials" in size order, from smallest to longest. Ask, "why do you think you needed to use 8 unifix cubes to measure your foot, but only 3 large pegs?"

Suggested Themes: All About Me, Numbers

Thought of the day…
"Our greatest natural resource is the minds of our children."
—Walt Disney

Teacher Tips

Allow children to work with a partner as a cooperative learning experience. The teacher should know ahead of time which students will be partners so that no one is left out.

Twinkle, Twinkle Little Star

- Place several different big and small stars on the flannel board, and recite the poem, "Twinkle, Twinkle Little Star."

- Vocabulary building: Print the following words on cards—twinkle, star, above, diamond. Provide visual cues to help describe each word.
  — Explain that *twinkle* means the same as a shiny or sparkling light, and provide a glittery object to demonstrate the "twinkle."
  — Point to the stars on the flannel board, and ask "what are these things called? Where have you seen *stars*? What do you think they are made of?"
  — Give each child a paper star and ask the children to place the stars behind their backs, in front of their faces, next to their shoulders, *above* their heads.
  — Draw a *diamond* shape on the board and ask if anyone knows what it is called. Explain that it is a *diamond* shape, and see if anyone can find a *diamond* shaped object in the classroom. Ask, "does anyone know of any other type of *diamond*? There is a baseball *diamond*, where baseball players stand as they play the game. There is the *diamond* that is a shiny, sparkling rock, which is made into jewelry." Recite the poem again, and when you come to the part, "like a *diamond* in the sky," ask, "which *diamond* do you think they are talking about? The shape, the baseball *diamond*, or the sparkling rock?"

- Discussion question: What else can you see sparkling at night?

- Follow-up activity: Provide each child with black or dark blue construction paper and white or yellow tempera paint. Children create their own starry nights, painting big and small stars. (Some may "pattern" their big and small stars.) Let children sprinkle glitter onto wet paint, using the pincer grasp. Attach a copy of the poem to each starry painting.

Suggested Themes: Big and Small Things, Day and Night, Space or Air Transportation

Thought of the day...
"Don't belittle—be big."

Twinkle, Twinkle Little Star

Twinkle, twinkle little star, how I wonder what you are!

Up above the world so high, like a diamond in the sky.

Twinkle, twinkle little star, how I wonder what you are!

Teacher Tips

When asking children about the stars, be sure to accept all responses. Have non-fiction books about "stars" available so that you can help children find answers to their questions.

Discovery Activities

A Shape For Me

Get It Together

- Red and white finger paint.

- Large finger paint paper.

- Smocks.

- Scissors for each child.

Let's Get Started

- Using red finger paint, children paint on large finger paint paper.

- Allow children to paint for about five minutes with red paint only.

- Next add white finger paint to the child's paper.

- Ask the children to describe what is happening to the red paint (red paint is turning pink).

- Encourage children to draw different shapes with fingers, including circles, squares, triangles, ovals and hearts.

- When finger paint paper is dry the children cut out their favorite shapes.

Mind Stretchers

- For the developmentally young learner try adding a texture (gelatin powder) to the wet finger paint. Assist the children in forming basic shapes. When dry, cut out shapes. The child will use three of the five senses: smell, sight and touch. Use a marker to write the names of the shapes on paper.

- For the more advanced students suggest that they cut as many different shapes as they can. String the shapes together to make a finger-paint necklace.

Teacher Tips

It is better to finger paint with half of the class at one time, rather than attempting to paint and clean up with an entire class of four-year-olds. One group can finger paint while the other group is busy with another less messy activity. Some students may be hesitant to touch the paint. Provide cotton swabs, craft sticks, paint brushes, etc. for the students to use. As the students become more familiar with the paint and see others having fun, they will be more apt to try it. Do not scold or punish those that do not wish to touch the paints.

Tearing a Rainbow

Get It Together

- Tissue paper—at least 4 different colors (bright colors work best).

- Spray bottles.

- White vinegar (1/2 cup) and water (1/2 cup)—in each spray bottle.

- Sketch of a large rainbow—colors will be filled in with tissue paper.

- Paper and crayons.

- Watercolor paints.

Let's Get Started

- Have a large rainbow sketched on white mural paper with pencil. Ask children, "what is missing from our rainbow?" (Colors!)

- Divide the class into at least 4 groups, giving each group a specific color of tissue paper to tear. (If you have 5 bright colors of tissue paper, create 5 groups. One group will tear blue, one group will tear red, etc. Children can place tissue scraps in small bags until it is their turn to place on rainbow.)

- Children work at tables, drawing beautiful rainbows and colorful pictures, using crayons. After coloring rainbows, let them "write" about their rainbows. (Ask them to write about how their rainbows were formed or where they were found.) Rewrite their words, if they want you to. Then, let them use watercolors to paint over their rainbow pictures. The water on the waxy crayons makes a nice color effect. (Some may even notice the water "beading up."

- While they are working on this activity, follow the directions for the next step.

- As children work, call 1 color group at a time to the center of the circle, where sketched rainbow is on the floor. Children take turns, placing their colors onto *one section* of the rainbow. (Do not glue on—just place on top of white paper.) When the group has covered their section of the rainbow with tissue paper, let children spray the tissue lightly with water and vinegar. Use a spray bottle for this. (Don't soak, just wet enough to hold tissue in place.) Then, send those children back to their tables to work on rainbow pictures. Call another "color group" to place their tissue on another section of the rainbow. Spray lightly with water and vinegar to hold in place. Repeat until all color groups have been added to the rainbow.

- When the rainbow is filled with tissue, keep if flat on the floor and thoroughly spray with vinegar and water. (You can let children take turns spraying—helps to strengthen hand muscles.) Let the rainbow dry on the floor or other flat surface. When dry, the tissue will fall off, but the colors will have bled through to the white paper—creating a beautiful rainbow. (The water makes the colors bleed, and vinegar adds to the brilliance and helps set the color.)

- Bright or dark colors of tissue work best!

- Display rainbow on board, when dry. Hang children's individual "rainbow" pictures around it.

Teacher Tips

In order to work with the group that is placing their colors on the rainbow, have the remainder of the class work at the tables coloring rainbows with crayons and painting over them with watercolors. That activity can be done successfully with little teacher interaction. Remember to allow students to tear the tissue paper. Tearing helps strengthen the fingers for the pincer grasp which is needed for writing.

Tear It Up

Get It Together

- Variety of materials for tearing (tissue paper, construction paper, foil, wax paper, cardboard, newspaper, packing foam, tagboard, etc.).

- Mural paper or large poster board.

- Glue.

Let's Get Started

- Provide a wide variety of paper and other materials for children to tear.

- After children tear a certain material, ask if the material was *easy to tear* or *hard to tear*.

- Have each child make two separate piles of materials: *easy to tear* and *hard to tear*.

- When children are finished tearing, create class chart—"Easy to Tear;" "Hard to Tear," placing the sorted paper on the appropriate side of the chart.

Easy to Tear:	Hard to Tear:

Mind Stretchers

- For the developmentally young learner ask the student to tear the various papers and tell you if they were *hard* or *easy* to tear. No further classification or sorting is necessary.

- For the more advanced learner have the students sort materials into groups other than *hard to tear* or *easy to tear*. (Sort according to other attributes, for example: shiny and dull, colorful and dull, etc.)

Teacher Tips

This activity allows children to use their fingers to tear different types of materials in order to help develop eye hand coordination and finger strength. It also helps to develop critical thinking and scientific inquiry skills.

Shape It Up

Get It Together

- Sidewalk or concrete area.
- Sidewalk chalk.
- Small shape cards.
- Finger paints.
- Finger paint paper cut into large shapes (circle, square, rectangle, triangle).
- Smocks.

Let's Get Started

- Group 1: The adult draws 4 large shapes on the sidewalk: circle, square, rectangle, triangle. Working outside, children will pick a shape card and then find the same chalk shape on the ground. The child will stand inside the shape. Check to make sure the children find the same shape in which to stand. Ask the children if they can name the shapes in which they are standing. Collect shape cards, hand out new shape cards and repeat the activity.

- Group 2: Working inside, children choose a shape on which to finger paint (Have finger paint paper cut into large triangles, rectangles, squares, and circles). Have children choose 1, 2, 3, or all shapes to paint.

Mind Stretchers

- For developmentally young learners that are hesitant to put their fingers into the paint, allow them to use craft sticks, cotton swabs, etc. to experiment with the paint.

- For the more advanced student you can expand the number of shapes to include shapes such as ovals, a cross, etc.

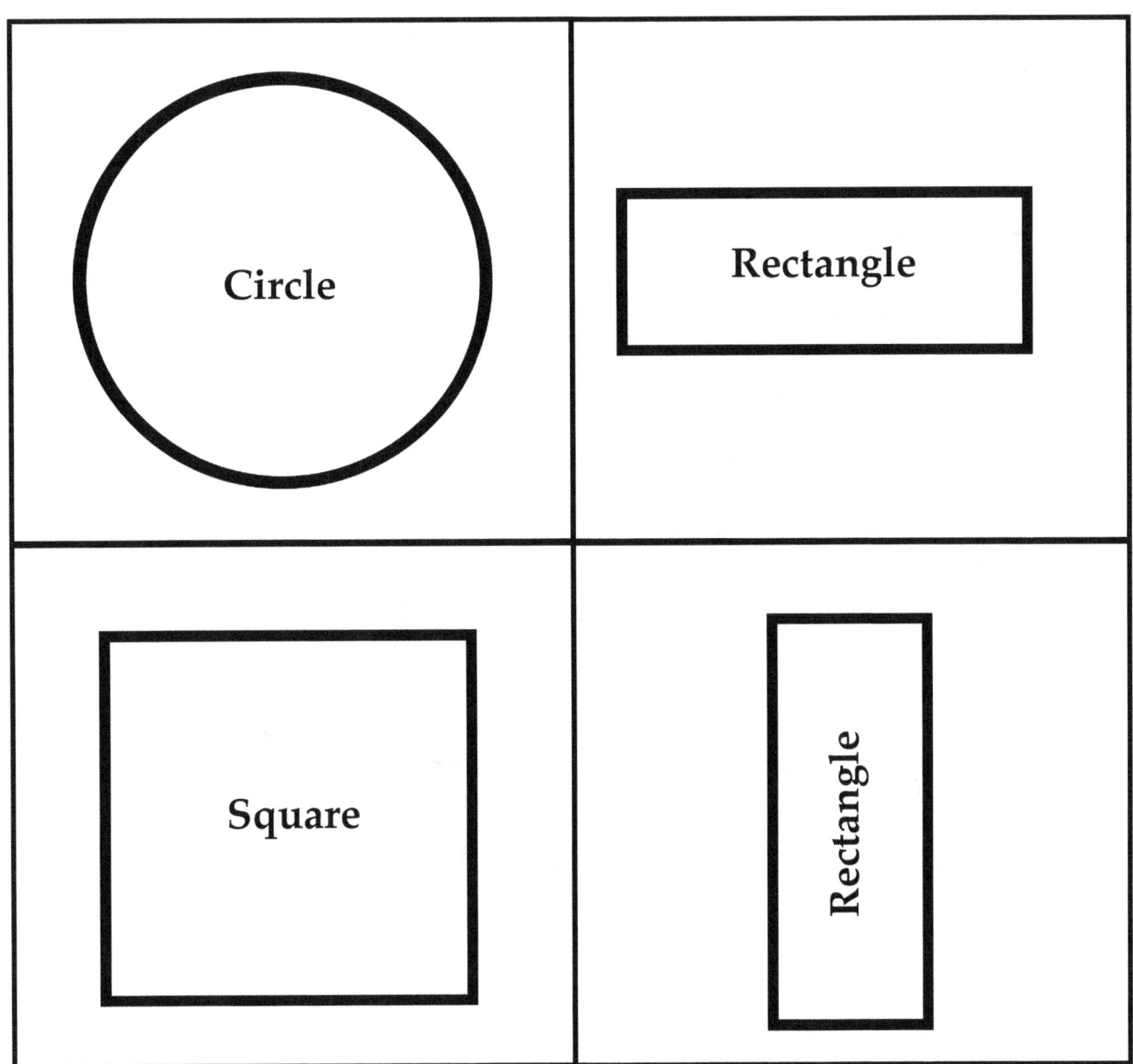

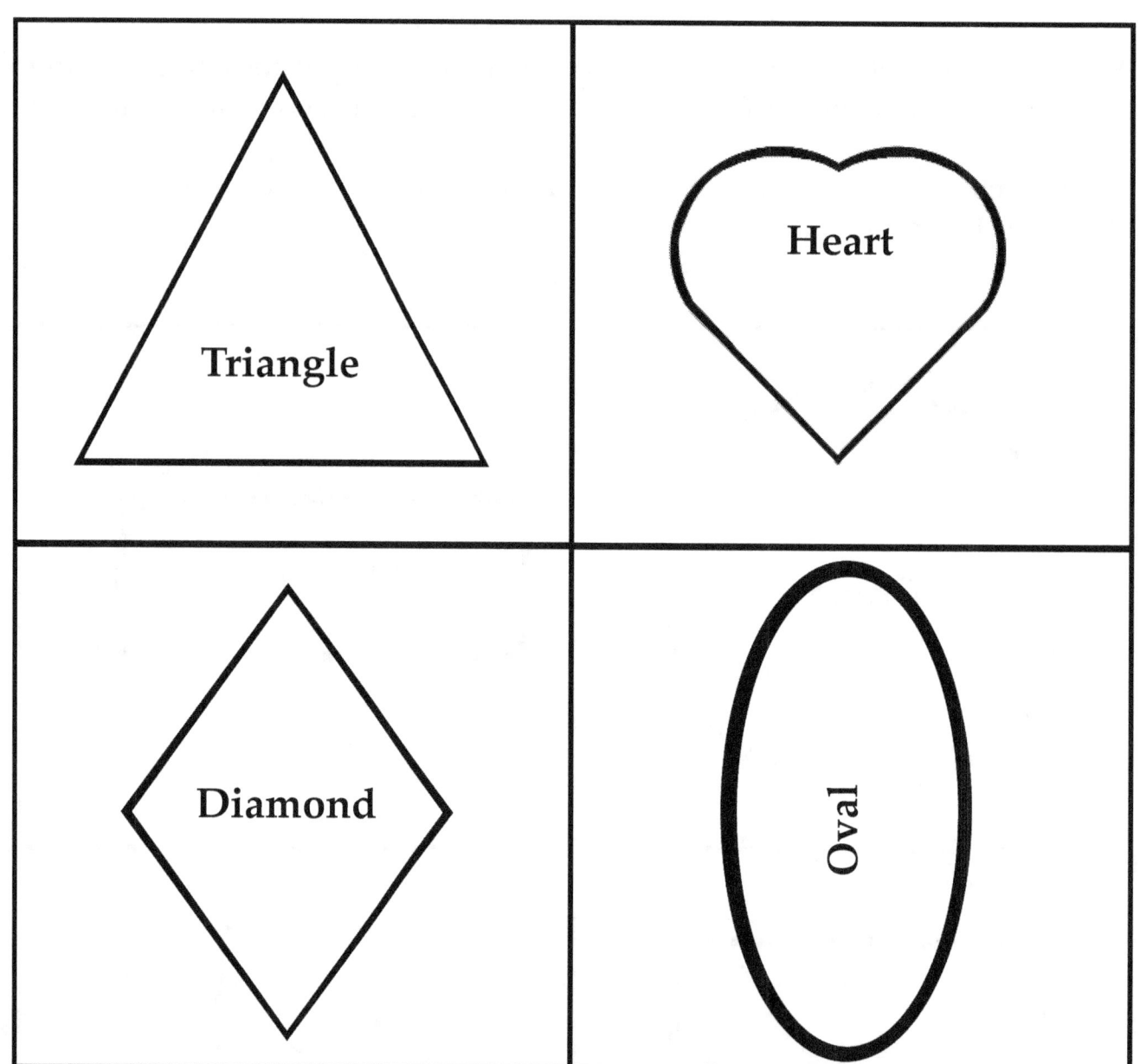

Teacher Tips

Divide the class into two groups. This activity works best with a smaller number of children, in order to provide each child with individual attention and to be able to access his or her knowledge of shapes.

Stop, Drop, and Roll

Get It Together

- Toy telephone.

- Board or chart paper.

- Several sets of the numbers 9-1-1 cut and taped to the tables.

Let's Get Started

- Discuss ways in which firefighters help us.

- Have children practice the "Stop, Drop, and Roll" sequence.

- Explain the importance of that sequence as it relates to fire safety.

- Write "9-1-1" on board or paper.

- Use a telephone to demonstrate how to call that number and report an emergency (emphasize calling 9-1-1 for emergencies only). Have children practice.

- Using sandpaper, or other textured paper, have the numbers 9-1-1 cut out and taped to tables.

- Children make crayon rubbings of the numbers 9-1-1.

Mind Stretchers

- For the developmentally young learners try having them trace the sandpaper numbers with their fingers, saying each number as they trace it.

- For the more advanced student try role playing various 9-1-1 situations. Have the student decide whether it is a true emergency or not.

Teacher Tips

The "Stop, Drop, and Roll" sequence refers to fire safety. Without startling the children, discuss what they need to do in the event that their clothing catches on fire. "Stop" means to stop whatever activity is happening, not to run, and to stand still. "Drop" means to carefully drop to the ground and "Roll" means to move from side to side to extinguish the flames.

Oobleck Activities

Get It Together

- Oobleck (see recipe).

- Cups, spoons, etc. for pouring, mixing, filling.

- Baggies to place leftover oobleck in (if using the oobleck for another day's activity).

Let's Get Started

- Make oobleck with the group. Measure, pour, and mix together.

- Discuss these properties with the children, and allow children to experience holding the *solid*, then watching the mixture drip from their hands like a *liquid*.

- Place the oobleck on wax paper for each child. (If you want to complete the remainder of this activity the next day, place the oobleck in zippered baggies for the next lesson).

- Children work with cups, spoons, nesting cups, etc. so they can pour and fill using the mixture.

- If a child is "sensory sensitive" and does not want to touch the mixture, provide craft sticks for the child to use in exploring the mixture.

Activity #2—"Goop" Racing

- Have each child put on a smock and gather outside with full bowls of oobleck.

- Ask the children, "what happens when you pick it up?" (Refer to previous lesson.)

- After discussing this, point out the empty buckets scattered around the outside play area.

- Tell them that they will be moving the oobleck (goop) from the full containers to the empty ones by using only their hands.

- As the children move the goop from full to empty containers some of the goop will fall to the ground. This will be easy to clean up, as it dissolves in water.

- Observe the children's reactions when the goop falls from their fingers before they reach the empty bowl. Do they run faster? Do they move the bowls closer? Do they try to work as a team? Do they try to pick up the goop?

- As the children experiment with the goop, play alongside them, keeping them focused on the goal of moving the goop from bowl to bowl.

- Model new ways of getting goop from bowl to bowl . (For example: Pass some from your hands to a child's hands.)

- Follow the children's cues (example: If they decide to work cooperatively and pass the goop from hand to hand, encourage them to do so).

- For easy clean up, bring out a hose or buckets of water. The oobleck will dissolve into the grass/sand and will disappear from the children's hands when water is added.

Oobleck Recipe

Materials Needed:

- 1 ½ cup corn starch.
- 1 cup water.
- Food color (optional).

- Mix the ingredients together. When "pushed" together the mixture will appear dry and solid. As children let go of the mixture it will flow like a smooth liquid.

Teacher Tips

Oobleck should NOT be prepared in advance of the lesson. The children need to experience how the materials look and feel. After following the recipe, the mixture should be able to form a solid and should also drip like a liquid. Adjust the recipe as needed to maintain that consistency.

Mouse House

Get It Together

- Inch cubes and unifix cubes.

- Mice counters (or similar counters).

- 2 small wooden dice (number cubes).

Let's Get Started

- Children use small inch cubes and unifix cubes to build "houses." Each will roll a die (small with numerals) to determine how many mice may live *inside* his house. The child counts out that number of mice counters and places them inside. Then he/she rolls the die again to determine how many mice live *outside* the house. The child may arrange furniture inside the house, providing 1 chair for each mouse. The adult moves to and talks to each child as he works.

Mind Stretchers

- For the developmentally young learner present the concept of "inside" and "outside" in isolation. Do not introduce both concepts during the same activity. Focus on just one.

- For the more advanced learner ask higher level questions such as, "How many animals would you have inside if one left the inside of the house and was added to the backyard outside? How many animals would you have outside if one left and went inside? Do you have more animals inside or outside? How could you get the same number of animals inside and outside?"

Teacher Tips

Divide students into groups of no more than 4. Implementing this activity in a large group setting will be ineffective, will lose instructional momentum, and may also lend itself to students acting out.

Germy Germs

Get It Together

- Chart prepared for each group.
- Cooking oil.
- Paper towels.
- Bucket of water.
- Liquid soap.

Let's Get Started

- Ask, "Why is it important to wash our hands?" Brainstorm, using a chart divided into two columns. One column will be labeled, "Why do we wash our hands?" The other column will be labeled, "What could we use to clean our hands?" Record children's responses.

- Mention that hands have germs. If we touch food with our hands and germs get on our food, those germs could make us sick.

- Ask the children to inspect their hands. Ask, "do you see any germs?" Have the students look at their fingernails. Ask them if they see any dirt under their fingernails. Stress the fact that germs live in dirt. The children can see dirt, but they cannot see germs.

- Use an eye-dropper and drop 1 or 2 drops of cooking oil onto each student's hand. Have students rub the oil into their hands. Tell them to pretend the "oil" is a bunch of germy germs.

- Discuss ways to get the germs (oil) off their hands. Give each child a paper towel and have him/her wipe away the oil. Ask the children if all of the oil came off.

- Let each child try washing his/her hands with only water. Ask again, "did all the oil come off?"

- Place a few drops of liquid soap on the children's hands. Ask them to rub the soap all over their hands, being sure to clean every spot. Have children rub their hands in water to rinse the soap. Stress the importance of rubbing their hands together as they wash. Ask them if the oil came off.

- Explain that just like the oil, germs need soap, water, and the rubbing of hands together to get rid of them. Teach them to lather and rub hands together while singing to themselves *The Happy Birthday Song* (or the alphabet song). By the time they have finished singing, the germs should all be washed away.

Mind Stretchers

- For the developmentally young learner shorten the lesson by asking the child to inspect his or her hand for any germs. Mention that germs cannot always be seen. Brainstorm ways to wash our hands (ex: Use soap and water, rub hands together, dry hands with a clean paper towel).

- For the more advanced learner extend the lesson by giving various situations when hand washing is critical (ex: after touching animals, after sneezing, after being on the playground, playing in the dirt, etc.). Tell them that to get their hands really clean they need to use soap and water and lather their hands for two minutes. This can be timed by singing (to themselves) *The Happy Birthday Song*. When they are finished singing, they are done washing their hands.

Outside Activity

- Play "germ, germ, soap." Follow the same rules for Duck, Duck, Goose. Explain that soap chases the germs away.

Teacher Tips

Because it is not possible for every child to use the sink at the same time, provide other types of soapy water in buckets, pails, or in the water table.

Eight Germs

Get It Together

- Counters (at least 8).

- A piece of paper for each child.

- Small paper rectangle (pink, green, or red).

Let's Get Started

- Each child will count 8 counters or small cubes to place on a piece of 8" x 11" paper.

- Tell the children that the counters represent "germs" and cannot be moved off the paper.

- Tell them the following story (adapt it as necessary):

8 Little Germs

There were 8 little germs living in a city (the paper represents the city). They were all the best of friends and they did everything together. They went to school together (children move their group of 8 to "pretend" schools on their paper). They went to the grocery store together (children move their group of 8 to a "pretend" store); they even lived together (children move their group of 8 to a "pretend" house).

One afternoon the mayor of the town brought in a bar of soap to clean the city (each child receives a small rectangle—blue, yellow, or pink—to use as the bar of soap.) "There are so many germs in this city!" exclaimed the mayor. "It is time to use the soap to get rid of them. I'm going to wash the middle of this city."

(Children place the "soap" in the middle of the paper.) The eight germs heard this and decided to leave the middle of the city and hide from the soap. The germs left the city but not together. Some went to the top of the town and some went to the bottom of the town. (Ask each child to count the number of germs on top and the number on the bottom. After counting say, "5 plus 3 equals 8," etc. Point to the counters as you describe the equation.)

The mayor decided to wash the top of the city. The germs that were on the top quickly ran to the left and right sides of the city. How many germs on the right side? How many on the left side? (After the child counts and tells you the number of germs on each side of the city, put the numbers in an equation again. Point to the counters).

The mayor knew the germs were still in the city hiding. So he washed the whole town with soap from top to bottom, and from right to left. How many germs were left in town?

The children respond, "zero" and brush all the "germs" off their towns.

Mind Stretchers

- For the developmentally young learner review the story without acting out every step. Focus on beginning with 8 "germs" and ending with zero. Teach the children to count each germ as they touch it, using one-to-one correspondence.

- For the more advanced learner, ask, "How many ways can we make 8?" Place 1 germ on the paper. "How many more germs do we need to make 8?" Count out 7 more, keeping them separate from the 1. Repeat for numbers 2-7.

SOAP

"Germ Town"

Teacher Tips

This lesson introduces the concept of addition. In order to keep it age-appropriate, simply state, "5 + 3 = 8" as the children move their counters. It is not necessary to write the equation and teach the mathematical symbols at this age.

Doctor Doctor

Get It Together

- A large bag containing a doll or stuffed animal for each child.

- Masking tape, craft sticks, doctor's kit, bandages, etc.

Let's Get Started

- Discuss ways in which doctors help us.

- Bring a bag filled with dolls and/or stuffed animals to present to the group.

- Pretend you hear crying sounds from inside the bag.

- Pull a doll or stuffed animal from the bag, placing it near your ear.

- Tell the children that the doll whispered to you that he/she is sick.

- Bring out the "pretend" medical supplies.

- Ask the children for ideas about how they could help the sick doll.

- Have the children act out some of their ideas.

- Let them know that you still hear more dolls crying in the bag.

- Give each child a doll or stuffed animal to fix.

- Watch to see the materials the children select as they work on their "sick" dolls. Do they give their dolls tender care, or do they repeatedly give shots with the syringe? Are they capable of opening the bandages? Do they work as a team or individually? Listen for the language they use. Encourage the children who lose interest in their dolls to "doctor" you or a willing classmate.

- At the closing of the activity go around the room and ask the children's dolls/stuffed animals if they feel better. (For example: "I noticed you had a sore arm. Are you feeling better?") Listen closely as the children respond to your questions.

Mind Stretchers

- For the developmentally young learner try having them hold the doll, talking sweetly to it, comforting it, and reassuring it.

- For the more advanced student try having the student identify other materials that could be used in a doctor's office and what their use could be. Provide small pads of paper and pencils and ask children to write "prescriptions" of needed medications.

Teacher Tips

While involved in this activity it is not uncommon for children to make reference to private body parts. If this happens, treat it "matter of factly" and do not dwell on the comment. Simply redirect and move on.

Create Your Own Germ

Get It Together

- Paper and a variety of art materials (ex: watercolors, craft sticks, pom-pons, sequins, tissue paper, coffee filters, yarn, pipe-cleaners, etc.).

- Glue.

- Scissors.

Let's Get Started

- Act out the story of "Two Friendly Hands" with the entire group before moving to tables to work.

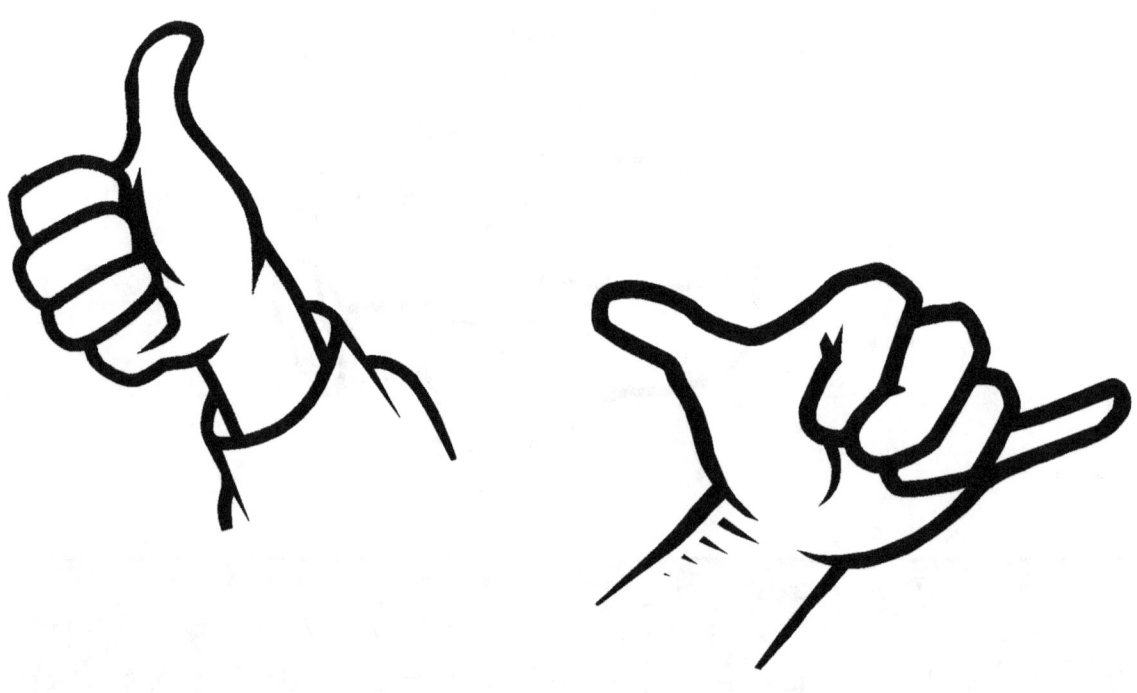

Two Friendly Hands

"Once upon a time there was a happy hand. This hand led a simple life and kept himself physically fit by exercising everyday. His favorite activity was aerobics."

(Hold up your right fist and encourage students to do the same. Make a fist with the hand you are holding up. Using your pointer finger do finger aerobics while humming a catchy tune. Children should exercise their hand too).

"Whew this is hard work…. OK. Just five more. One, two, three, four five." (Stop the finger aerobics.)

"Oh, I forgot to mention that our hand can also count to five using his fingers." (Count to five holding up one finger at a time.)

"While counting one afternoon, Hand discovered that he could do something else. He could use his number one finger to point."

"He pointed to the door." (Point to the door.)

"He pointed to the window." (Point to the window.)

"He pointed to wonderful student work." (Point to student work that is displayed.)

"Hand really loved to point. He pointed everyday, all day, until something fabulous happened."

"HE SNAPPED!" (Snap your fingers several times.)

"Can you hear that snap? Hand was so proud of the new noise he could make!"

"Hand really wanted to share the fun with his best friend who lived across the street. So he waved toward his friend's house." (Wave)

"After a lot of waving, his friend finally came outside." (Hold up your left hand.)

"Happy to see his friend, Hand waved back." (Both hands face each other, waving.)

"The two hands were the best of buddies. They liked to do the same things. They loved to exercise." (Making a fist with both hands, do finger aerobics with both pointer fingers.)

"The two hands also made music together and applauded their efforts." (Clap several times.)

"AAAAAA-CHOOOOO!"

"Oh no, Hand was sick."

"Now both Hand and his friend were really sad. They had a big problem. Can anyone tell me what their problem was?" (Elicit the response that Hand had sneezed germs on his friend.)

"What would happen if Hand touched his friend? His friend would get the germs and could get sick. Hand and his friend could not make music together because Hand was covered with germs. How do you think they solved this problem?"

(Elicit the responses that Hand should have sneezed into his shoulder or elbow and not his hand. Hand should have washed, using soap and water to get rid of the germs)

"The good news is that Hand did wash and he did use soap and water. Now he and his friend could play together again." (Clap hands together.)

- Ask the children to describe what they think a "germ" might look like.

- Explain that a special tool called a "microscope" is needed to see germs and even though we can't see them, they are there.

- Allow children to creatively express themselves by making their own germs.

- Provide a variety of art materials for the students to work with.

- Display their handmade germs on a board with the following caption neatly printed, "Germs, Germs, Go Away! Soap and Water Will Wash You Away."

Mind Stretchers

- For the developmentally young learner ask the students what they think a germ might look like. Draw their responses on a large piece of paper.

- For the more advance learner ask the child to describe his or her germ. Record the responses and ask the child to repeat the response to you.

Teacher Tips

When creating their "germs" it is important to provide many different types of materials. Encourage each child's individual creativity and focus on the process rather than the product. As the students are working, visit with each child, asking him or her to explain their creation.

Cover Your Sneeze

Get It Together

- Small paper plates.

- Art materials for making faces.

- Paper and scissors (for tracing and cutting hands).

- Staplers and tape.

- 1 tissue (or small napkin) per child.

- Glue

Let's Get Started

- Children make faces, bodies, and arms that fold, in order to "catch a sneeze" with a tissue.

- Children decorate small paper plates for heads, using yarn and other art materials for hair and faces.

- Staple heads to rectangular bodies (tagboards approximately 8" x 11").

- Tape or staple arms to bodies (thin rectangles).

- Children trace and cut out their hands, then tape them to their arms.

- In 1 hand each child will glue a tissue or napkin. When the arm is bent up to the face it should "cover the sneeze" with the tissue.

- Ask each child, "Why is the tissue in the hand?"

- Print the response on the body.

Mind Stretchers

- For the developmentally young learner try just making the face out of a paper plate (rather than making the entire body). Children decorate the plate to look like a face. Glue a napkin or tissue over the mouth to represent covering a sneeze.

- For the more advanced learner discuss other ways to prevent sickness from spreading (ex. cover your sneeze, wash your hands, etc.).

Teacher Tips

As children are creating their bodies allow them to use any colors they choose. For example, if they give themselves purple hair, readily accept that. Children at this age do not consider skin color and often will select their favorite color for their skin, hair, eyes etc.

Cleared For Landing

Get It Together

- Numerals 1-5 on floor.

- Numerals 1-5 on cards for children to hold.

- Chairs arranged in rows to replicate the inside of an airplane.

Let's Get Started

- Create 5 "runways" in the front of your classroom with large numbers 1-5 on each. (You can use large white bulletin board paper with dotted lines down the center, each strip is labeled with the number 1, 2, 3, 4, or 5).

- Give 5 children a number 1-5.

- Recite "Cleared for Landing."

- Have those 5 children land on the runways that match their numbers.

- They land as their number is called.

- Repeat so that all children have a turn to land on the runway.

Poem: Cleared for Landing

Five little airplanes flying in the sky.
Come in for a landing from up so high.

The first little airplane shining in the sun,
Is the first to land on runway number one.

The second little airplane carrying the crew,
Lands very slowly on runway number 2.

The third little airplane is quite a sight to see,
It lands quietly on runway number 3.

The fourth little airplane can wait no more,
And lands very quickly on runway number 4.

The fifth little airplane is the last to arrive,
And finally it lands on runway number 5!

Mind Stretchers

- For the developmentally young learner try having only 2 landing strips instead of 5. Continue with the activity as described.

- For the more advanced learner use higher level questioning to promote critical thinking. For example, ask, "What if the 5th airplane did not arrive? How many planes would there be? What would happen if another airplane came to the airport? How many planes would there be?"

Teacher Tips

This is a circle time or large group activity. Five students at a time will act out the poem while the others recite the poem. Repeat three or four times so that all students have a chance to act out the poem.

Astronaut Training Center

Get It Together

- Hula hoops.

- Jump ropes.

- Sidewalk chalk.

- Outside play area.

Let's Get Started

- Create an "astronaut training center" in an outside area.

- Place a chalk line on the sidewalk and call it a "moonbeam."

- Children practice walking on the moon beam in a variety of ways. They can tip toe, hop, walk softly, etc.

- Tie a few jump ropes around small chairs and have children jump over and/or crawl under ropes.

- Place hula hoops on the ground and pretend they are "craters" on the moon. Children jump from crater to crater.

Mind Stretchers

- For the developmentally young learner adjust this activity to meet individual needs. For example, some children may not yet be able to jump. Instead, they could crawl.

- For the more advanced learner have children describe spatial words as to what they are doing (ex. jumping OVER the hoop, standing NEXT TO the rope, crawling UNDER the chair, etc.).

Teacher Tips

When setting up the obstacle course be sure to set up a beginning point and ending point. The students will move through the activities in a sequential order.

Big, Small, Big, Small

Get It Together

- Unit blocks or other classroom materials that come in big and small sizes (examples include duplos, animal counters, bristle blocks, etc.).

- Play-doh.

- Safety scissors for each student.

Let's Get Started

Group 1:
- Demonstrate how to create an AB pattern using big and small blocks. Place a big block on the floor and then a small block next to it. Point to the big and small blocks, saying, "Big, small, big, small."

- Place another big and small block next to the first pair, in a line. Point to each block as you say, "Big, small, big, small. What comes next?" (Try changing your voice, to assist auditory learners. When saying "big," use a big, deep voice; when saying "small," use a soft, little voice.)

Group 2:
- Provide children with play-doh and ask them to create "big/small" patterns using play-doh.

- Provide safety scissors, so children can cut small pieces of play-doh.

- Have each child point to his/her play-doh pieces, saying "Big, small, big, small, etc."

Mind Stretchers

- For the developmentally young learners give them time to create "big/small" patterns out of classroom materials before working with play-doh. When children are ready to work with play-doh, allow them first to create big/small balls of play-doh before adding scissors. Once the children are able to produce an AB pattern out of big and small pieces of play-doh, provide safety scissors.

- For the more advanced students see if children can create an ABB pattern, using "big, small, small" pieces of play-doh.

Teacher Tips

This activity is designed to use with two groups at the same time. Children will work on each activity for approximately 10 minutes, then they will trade activities.

I Can Write!

Get It Together

- Children gathered at Circle Time.

- Large chart paper.

- Markers.

Let's Get Started

- Once you have established the developmental writing levels of the children by observing their attempts at writing, this activity is most useful. (Look to see which children can correctly print their names, which are attempting to write letters, and which are at the scribble-stage of writing.)

- Tell the children how much you enjoy seeing them trying to write about their drawings. Explain that we all write differently, and the important thing is that everybody "tries."

- Ask for a volunteer to come up to your chart to write something. Call on a child who may be mixing letters with shapes and other scribbles as he/she writes. Have that child use a marker to write on the chart paper, in front of his/her classmates. Be sure to praise the child's attempt at writing.

- Ask the child, "What did you write about?" After the child "reads" what he/she has written, write the spoken words beneath the writing. Say, "This is the way I write, and this is the way he/she writes," pointing to the writing.

- Ask for another volunteer to come up to the chart to write. This time, choose a child who is not writing letters, but uses scribbles. (If others giggle, remind the class how proud you are of this child, for coming forward to show everyone how he/she writes. Positively reinforcing his/her efforts will put a stop to the teasing.)

- Repeat Step 4, asking the child to "read" what he/she has written.

- Ask for one more volunteer to come up and write. Choose a child who is able to write his/her name. Then repeat Step 4.

- Save the chart paper, and continue with this when you have a few minutes between activities, or at the end of the day. Be sure to give all children a turn, if they want. When all children have had a turn, print the "date" on the paper, and hang it in the corner of the classroom, perhaps near the Writing Area. Start a new piece of chart paper, approximately one month later, following the same steps. Notice changes the children have made. Continue charting writing growth and sharing the results with the class. They will learn to be proud of their writing!

Teacher Tips

This activity is useful at the beginning of the year as it provides a motivation for writing and encourages all children to attempt writing. Praise every attempt at writing no matter how simplistic.

Look What I Can Do Now!

Get It Together

- One large piece of drawing paper for each child, folded in half, with a line drawn on the fold.

- On the left side of the fold, print the words: "When I was a baby, I could _____."

- On the right side of the fold, print the words: "Now that I am in preschool, I can _____."

- Crayons.

- Pencils.

Let's Get Started

- Children draw pictures on each side of the fold to complete the sentences.

- Children can complete the sentences themselves by trying to write their own words in the blanks. Adults should ask each child to read what he/she has written, and then offer to write beneath the child's words, if the child wants.

Teacher Tips

When taking a child's dictation, it is important to position yourself next to the child, as if the child were actually the one writing. The child needs to see you form letters from left to right. This cannot be accomplished if you are sitting in front of the child, or if you have positioned yourself anywhere except directly next to the child.

Our Favorite Colors

Get It Together

- White or manila construction paper.

- Variety of magazines (for children to cut).

- Variety of art materials (paper and/or fabric scraps, feathers, pom-pons, glitter, markers, yarn pieces, etc.).

- Variety of found materials (bottle tops, buttons, cardboard tubes, packing popcorn, acorns, twigs, small stones, shells, etc.).

- Glue.

- Safety scissors.

Let's Get Started

- Tell children they will design a picture using only one color—their favorite color!

- Have a variety of materials available. Provide different shades of one color, for example, light blue tissue paper, medium blue bottle tops, dark blue yarn.

- Children glue items onto white paper.

- Print the following words on each paper: "My favorite color is ____." When the child identifies his/her favorite color, print the color word on the line using either a marker or a crayon that matches the child's favorite color.

- Point to the words as you read, "My favorite color is red," and ask the child to "read" it back to you.

Mind Stretchers

- For the developmentally young try displaying colored materials in sorted piles, so the children will have an easier time focusing on one color. For example, all red materials should be grouped together, all blue should be together, etc. Offer a limited number of colors from which the children may choose, such as the three primary colors: red, blue, and yellow.

- For the more advanced students point out different shades of the same color, and ask, "which do you like better, light blue or dark blue?" The students may also draw, using their favorite colored markers or crayons.

My favorite color is _____.

Teacher Tips

The children may all select one or two colors, or they may all select a different color. Make sure that you have available plenty of materials if either situation should occur.

Necklace For My Secret Pal

Get It Together

- Several small, pre-cut shapes for patterning. (If children are just beginning to pattern, begin with 2 different shapes of the same color, or 2 different colors of the same shape. For example, use red circles and squares, or blue and yellow circles. This way, only 1 attribute is different, making it easier for them to pattern.)

- Long piece of yarn. (Prepare one end of the yarn by dipping the ends in glue, and allowing to dry overnight. The glue will cause the yarn to stiffen, making it easier for children to grasp and string. Another way to prepare the yarn for stringing is to tape one end tightly, to resemble a shoe lace. Children can grasp the tape while stringing.)

- Tissue paper or wrapping paper.

- Scotch tape.

- Construction paper, index cards, sticky notes, or note cards.

- Pencils or markers.

Let's Get Started

- Have each child's name printed on a piece of paper, folded and placed in a "secret bag." (If the children use picture symbols to represent themselves, use those symbols also so children will know which friend they chose. For example, if a child is the class "butterfly," place the butterfly on the paper, along with the child's name. This way, another child choosing this paper will know exactly which friend was chosen.)

- Place all names in a secret bag. You may use the whole group, or divide the class into 2 smaller groups. If you use 2 small groups, you will need 2 secret bags. Each child reaches in and picks a paper to read. Ask the children not to tell who their "secret pal" is.

- Children work at their tables, using hole-punchers to make holes in paper shapes.

- Children place shapes on the yarn, creating a necklace for their secret pal. Teach children to create an "AB" pattern, by choosing one shape, then the other, and then continuing with that pattern. Say, "triangle, circle, triangle, circle, what comes next?"

- When the children have finished stringing their shapes, tie the ends of the yarn together, forming a necklace.

- Children wrap their gifts, using tissue paper or wrapping paper and tape.

- Children write their names on the note cards or other papers, so their friends will know who their secret pals are!

- Exchange gifts at circle time, at the end of day, or during a celebration.

Mind Stretchers

- For the developmentally young learner have the children place the shapes in front of themselves on the table before stringing. This makes the pattern more visible before they string the shapes onto the necklaces. Ask the child to point to each shape as he/she says, "Circle, square, circle, square," or, "Yellow, blue, yellow, blue."

- For the more advanced students, see if they are able to create an "A,B,B" pattern. For example, have the children place the following shapes in front of themselves: circle, triangle, triangle, circle, triangle, triangle. See if they know what comes next, then allow them to string the shapes onto the necklace.

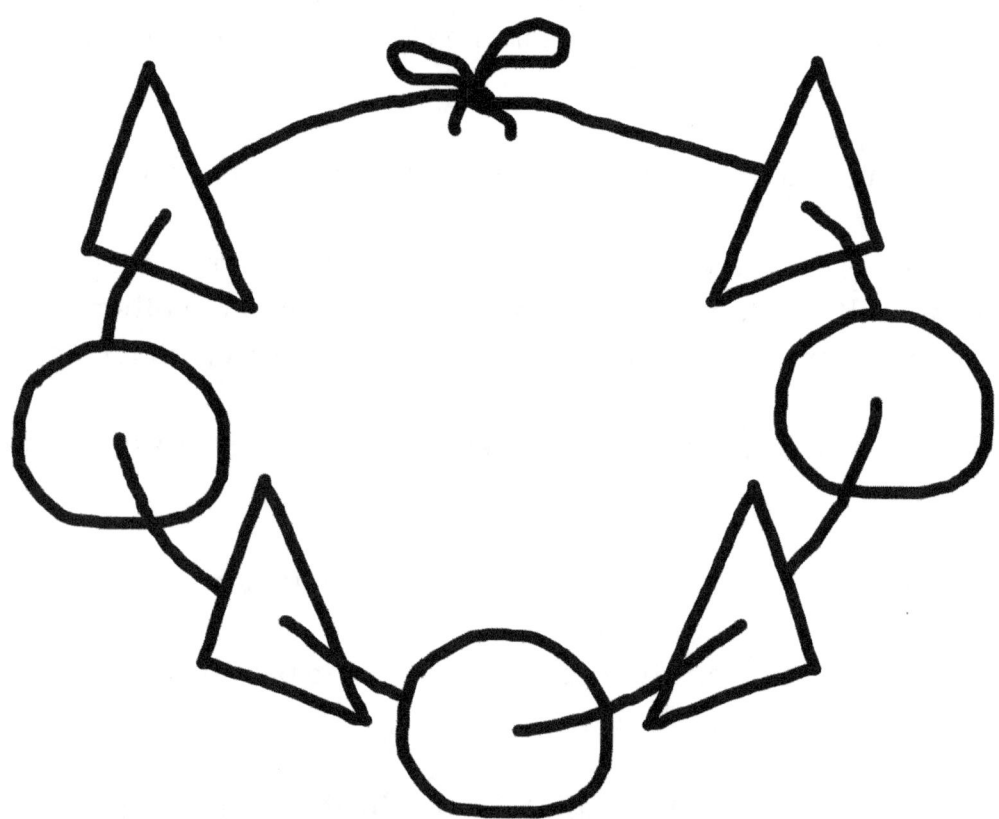

Teacher Tips

Discuss what a "secret pal" is and how much fun it would be to receive a gift from a secret pal while not knowing the identify of that person. Explain that grown ups often do this at parties, and teachers sometimes do it with other teachers in the school to celebrate special occasions and to have fun.

Share-A-Brush

Get It Together

- 1 large piece of paper for 2 children.

- Paint.

- 1 paintbrush per pair of children.

- Paint smocks.

Let's Get Started

- Discuss the word "sharing." Ask, "What are some things we can share with a friend?"

- Place children in pairs, providing 1 brush and 1 piece of paper for each pair.

- Watch the pairs. See if they can figure out a system to share the brush. If not, assist the pair, encouraging them to problem-solve as much as possible. (Ask, "Who would like to make the first line with the paintbrush?" "Now it is your turn to make the next line." If both children insist on being first to paint, ask one child to be the first to paint at the top of the paper and the other could be the first at painting the bottom of the paper. With encouragement, they can learn to share the rest of the paper.)

- When the pairs have finished painting, ask them to think of a "name" for their picture. Print the name on a card or sentence strip, along with the name of each child in the pair, and attach it to the painting. Display in the classroom.

Mind Stretchers

- For the developmentally young learner try counting to five while one child paints. Count "1, 2, 3, 4, 5, now it's Joey's turn." Then, when Joey has the brush, repeat the counting. Continue until the pair can share independently, or have each member of the pair count for the other.

- For more advanced students, ask the pair to take turns describing their painting to the rest of the class.

Teacher Tips

The important part of this lesson is that one brush should be shared between two children. If more than one color of paint is used, one brush should be in each container of paint. If only one color of paint is used, the children will need to be instructed on how to rinse the brush before dipping into another color.

Invent-An-Insect

Get It Together

- Paper.

- Crayons.

- Safety scissors.

- Glue.

- Variety of art and found materials such as pipe-cleaners, yarn bits, pom-pons, tissue paper, craft sticks, glitter, bottle tops, cardboard tubes, buttons, etc.

Let's Get Started

- Children trace around one of their own feet (with shoes on) using crayons.

- Children cut out the traced feet.

- Each child counts, or creates, 6 legs and 2 antennae, since those are two features of an insect. They place the legs and antennae around the cut-out feet, turning them into "insects."

- Children use a variety of materials to decorate the bodies of their insects.

- Have each child describe his insect. Is it a crawling or flying insect? Is it helpful or harmful? Where does your insect live?

Mind Stretchers

- For developmentally young children assist with the tracing of their feet. If children are able to cut with safety scissors, let them glue their insect bodies to paper for easy handling of materials. If children are not able to cut with scissors, they can simply decorate their traced feet, without cutting them out. Ask each child, "Does your insect crawl, or fly?"

- Let children draw or paint scenery to go along with their insects. Can the insects be found near flowers, ponds, in the ground, or in the kitchen? Children can also "name" their insects, and "write" about them.

Teacher Tips

Observe children as they cut. Remind them that their thumb should be "up," or on top, as they use the scissors.

What's Living in My Pond?

Get It Together

- Mural paper.

- Blue and green paint.

- Smocks and paintbrushes.

- Variety of art materials to use for completing "pond mural."

- Construction paper, scissors and glue.

Let's Get Started

- This is a two-day project. The first day the children will paint a large pond on white mural paper. Allow children to take turns adding to the blue pond water. The children will also need to paint tall grass and plant life around the pond.

- Ask the children to name all the insects and animals that would live in or near a pond.

- Children will use art materials to make the insects and animals for the pond. Encourage the children to use feathers, pipe cleaners, and wiggly eyes to create their pond life. Remember it is the *process* not the product that counts. If in doubt about what they have made, ask them to tell you about their creations. Make a label for each using lower case letters to help benefit the child's development.

- After allowing the mural to dry completely have children place their "Pond Life" creation on the mural.

- Allow the children to add the labels under their creations.

- Read the mural with the children from left to right.

Mind Stretchers

- For the developmentally young learner use pre-cut shapes that they can use to add wiggly eyes and glitter.

- For the more advance learner demonstrate how they can add more texture by putting their pond life creation on the sidewalk and rubbing over it with a crayon.

Teacher Tips

Before beginning this activity provide a number of books about pond life. This will help to build background knowledge. When asked to name various animals that live in or near a pond, students may respond with incorrect answers. If this occurs, refer them to a book about ponds and ask them if they can find this animal.

Musical-Share-A-Chair

Get It Together

- One chair for every child.

- Tape player/record player.

- Music.

Let's Get Started

- Ask the children if they've ever played "Musical Chairs." Line up chairs in a row, alternating the seats, placing one facing in and the next facing out, etc. Provide one less chair than the total number of children in the group. For example, if you have 18 children, provide 17 chairs.

- Demonstrate how children should walk around the chairs while playing.

- Play music for about 1 minute while watching the children move around the chairs.

- When the music stops, everyone must be touching a chair, sitting in someone's lap or touching hands. All children help to ensure that everyone is touching a chair or someone on a chair.

- After playing once, remove 1 or 2 chair(s). Remind the children that they'll all have to help each other share a chair once the music stops.

- Play music again and stop. Watch the children as they help each other find a chair or touch someone on a chair. Assist those who need help with "community building," etc.

- Depending on the size of the class, continue removing chairs until all of the children are huddled around 1 or 2 chairs. Praise the class for working so well together.

Teacher Tips

Children at this age do not understand competition. They play games simply for enjoyment. In this game everyone remains in the game for the purpose of creating a stronger community classroom.

Look at Beautiful Me!

Get It Together

- 1 piece of child-size mural paper for each child.

- Markers and crayons.

Let's Get Started

- Group children into pairs using a creative, fun way to select pairs. (For example, place several pairs of items in a bag. Ask each child to reach into the bag and pull out an item. After all the children have pulled an item from the bag, have the children find a friend with the same item. Those two children will work as partners.)

- One child in the pair lies on mural paper posing any way he/she likes.

- The other child traces around the partner using a marker.

- Both children decorate the body, drawing clothing, facial features, hair, eyes, ears, nose and mouth.

- After they have finished one body drawing, the other child lies on the mural paper and has his or her body traced. Both children add facial features, hair, and clothes. Adults can cut out and display the finished drawings.

Mind Stretchers

- For the developmentally young learner use body part cards to teach body parts. Run two copies and place them face down. Have children take turns trying to match body parts and correctly identify them. Suggested body parts to use are: hair, eyes, ears, nose, and mouth.

- For the more advanced students have them select a body part card and do not show it to the group. Give clues as to what it is (example: it is the part of the body you put a hat on, it is the part of the body that you put socks on etc).

Teacher Tips

Some students may make their body drawing anatomically correct. If this occurs remind children that they should decorate their bodies as if they were dressed in clothing. Praise the children who have drawn their body appropriately, rather than focusing on the students that may have not.

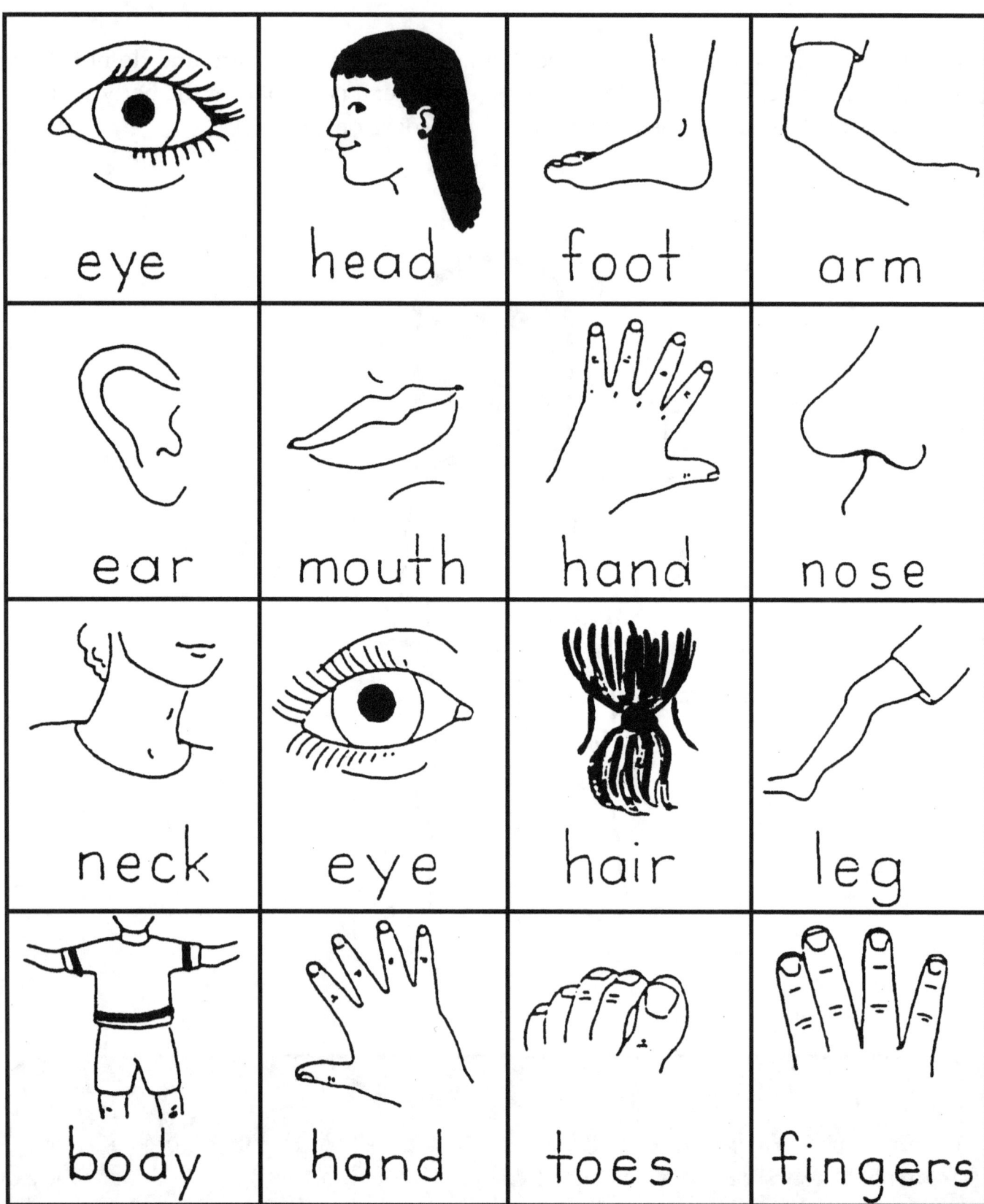

Little Boy Blue

Get it Together

- Activity sheet—"Little Boy Blue" 1 per child.

- Crayons.

- Toy farm animals.

Let's Get Started

- Recite "Little Boy Blue" nursery rhyme using flannel board pictures or other large pictures.

- Provide each child with a picture of "Little Boy Blue."

- Have children do the following:
    — Draw grass *between* the sheep and cow.

    — Draw a bird flying *over* the cow.

    — Draw a fence *next to* the cow.

    — Draw a feather *on* the hat of the boy.

- Ask, "Why would the sheep and cow need grass? Why are the birds flying? Why does the cow need a fence? Why does the boy need a hat? Would you like to work on a farm? Why or why not?"

Follow up: Sing and act out "I'm a Little Boy Blue" with your class.

"I'm a Little Boy Blue"

Sung to the tune of "Little Tea Pot"

I'm the little boy blue on the farm—(point to self)
I watch the sheep so they come to no harm—(Hand shading eyes looking for sheep)
I can get so tired that I sleep—(yawn)
Under the haystack fast asleep—(Hands together under head sleeping)

- For the developmentally young learner use toy farm animals to set up a farm. Name the animals.

- For the more advanced students try brainstorming other jobs the little boy could do for the farmer. The children can draw their favorite activity.

Thought of the day ...
"Never let the fear of striking out get in your way."
—George Herman "Babe" Ruth

Teacher Tips

During a movement and music activity, if a child is not willing to participate, allow him or her to remain seated and enjoy watching. Never force a child to stand up and participate in an activity in which he or she is uncomfortable.

Little Boy Blue, come blow on your horn.
The sheep's in the meadow, the cow's in the corn.
Where is the boy who looks after the sheep?
He's under the haystack, fast asleep.

Let It Melt

Get It Together

- 2 ice cubes for each child.

- Chart for making predictions: "Which will melt faster—A plain ice cube or an ice cube with salt on top?"

- Salt.

- Styrofoam trays or paper plates.

Let's Get Started

- Display 2 ice cubes that are the same size.

- Ask the children to describe how we get ice.

- Discuss "melting." Ask, "What do you think would make ice melt quickly?"

- Display regular table salt and ask children to make prediction: Which do you think will melt faster, plain ice or ice with salt on top?

- Use chart and ask the children to mark his/her prediction in the corresponding column—*Ice Cube* or *Ice cube with salt on top*.

- Provide 2 ice cubes on a styrofoam tray or paper plate, along with some table salt, for each child.

- Children sprinkle salt (use pincer grasp) on 1 cube. Nothing is added to the other cube.

- Ask why the ice cube with salt on it is melting faster than the cube without salt on it. (Adding salt makes it harder for water to freeze and causes ice cubes to melt faster).

Mind Stretchers

- For the developmentally young learner place ice cubes in the water table and allow the children to observe the ice melting in water.

- For the more advanced learner take the class outside and give each child an ice cube. Ask them to find ways to keep their ice cube from melting. Have the children share their findings.

Teacher Tips

When asking children to make their predictions about which ice cube will melt faster remind them that their answers are not wrong and that is how we learn.

Healthy Apples

Get It Together

- "My Apple Tree" booklet for each child.

- Crayons.

- Red finger paint.

Let's Get Started

- Provide children with "My Apple Tree" booklet—one page at a time.

- Children color trees.

- Using red finger paint, children use their pointer fingers to make the corresponding number of apples in each tree.

- Children also trace over the number on each page with red finger paint.

- When pages are dry, put pages of booklet together for each child.

Teacher Tips

If students are hesitant to touch the paint, they can make their apples in other ways. For example, provide cotton swabs, craft sticks, etc. for them to dip into the paint, or allow them to use another material besides paint, such as crumpled tissue paper as the apple.

My Apple Tree
by _____

apple

161

4 apples

5 apples

Fruit and Vegetable Bingo

Get It Together

- Fruit-Vegetable Bingo cards, one per child.

Let's Get Started

- Discuss the importance of eating healthy foods.

- Play fruits or vegetables bingo; children cover pictures using cubes or counters.

- First, try to fill row, and then try to fill the whole card.

- Continue playing until each child has a chance to fill a row or whole card (depending upon the game you're playing).

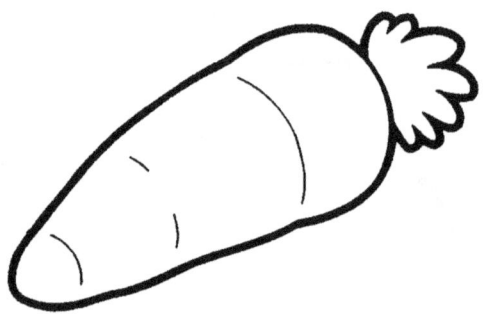

Teacher Tips

Children at this age do not understand competition. Therefore, it is important that there are no "winners" or "losers" and that all children have a chance to complete the task.

Fruit-Vegetable Bingo

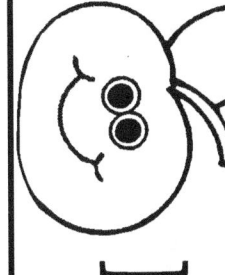

 pineapple	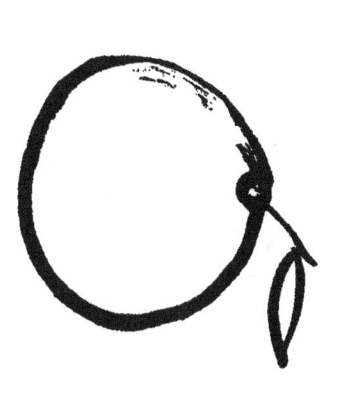 orange
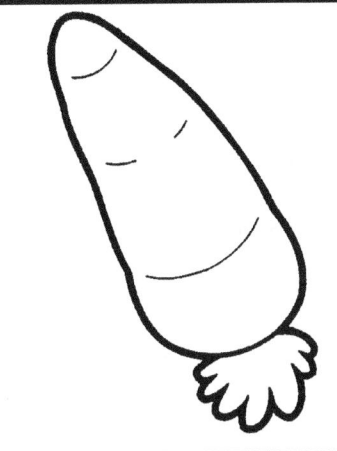 carrot	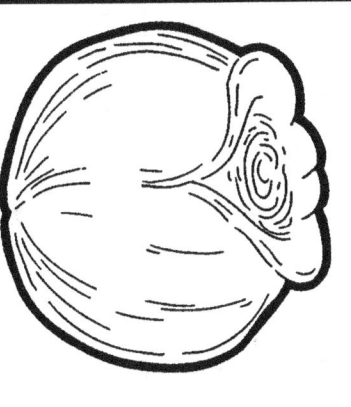 cabbage
 apple	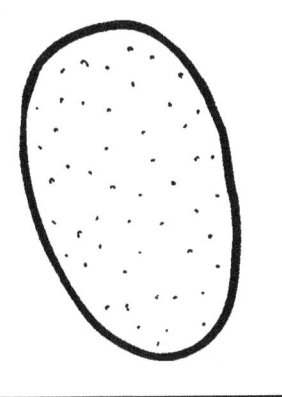 potato
 banana	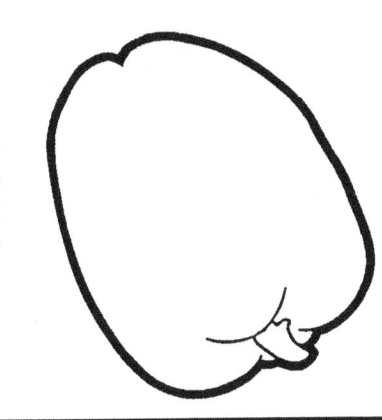 pepper

Fruit-Vegetable Bingo

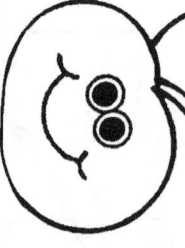

cabbage	potato
carrot	pineapple
corn	pepper
eggplant	tomato

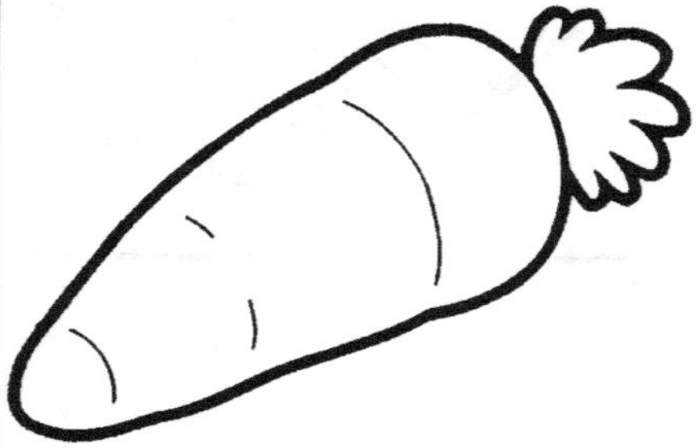

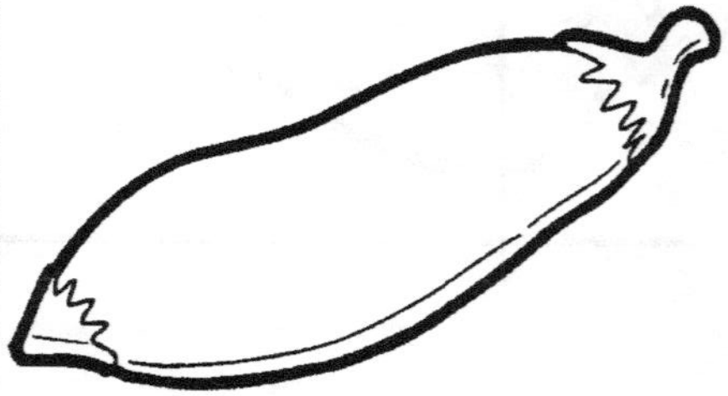

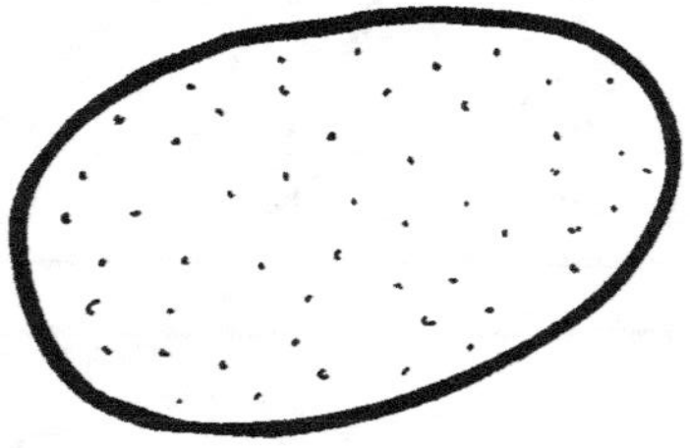

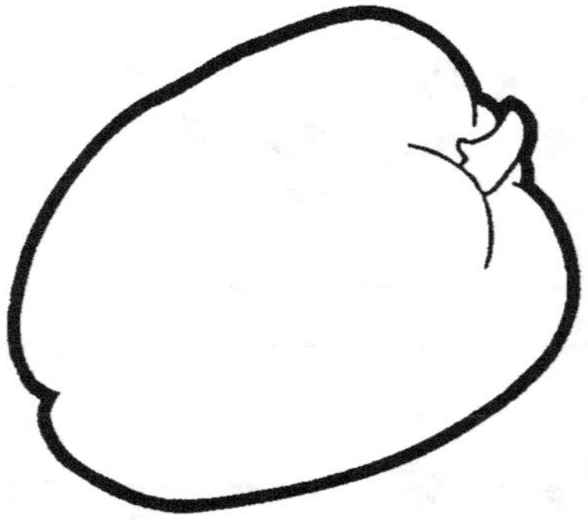

Fruit-Vegetable Bingo

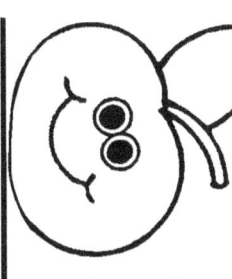

pineapple

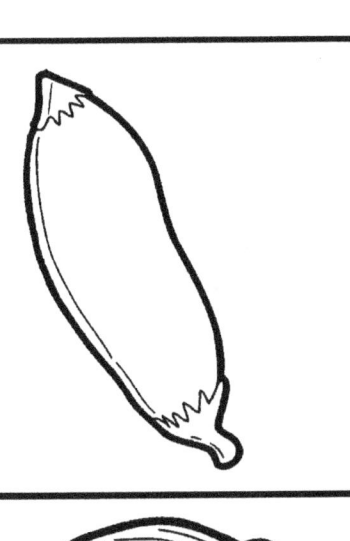
eggplant

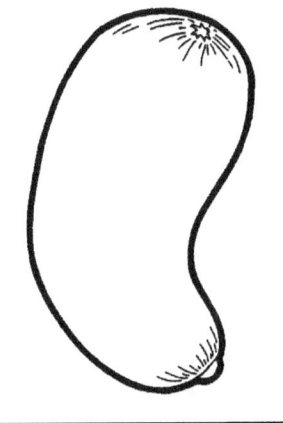
squash

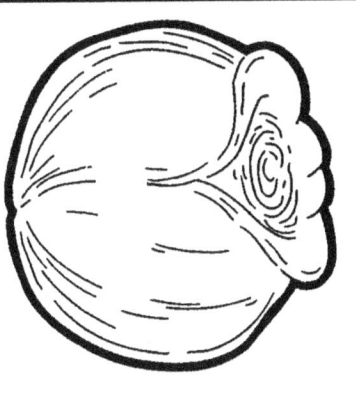
cabbage

corn

tomato

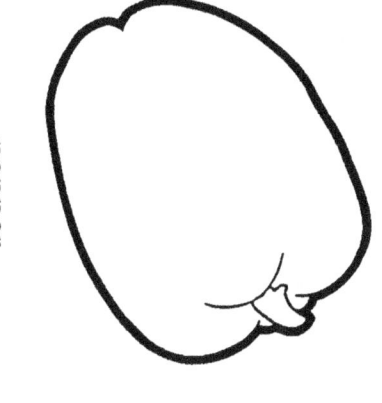
pepper

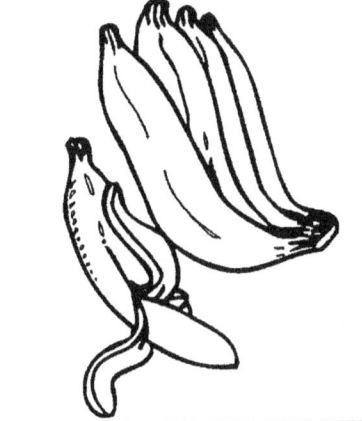
banana

Fruit-Vegetable Bingo

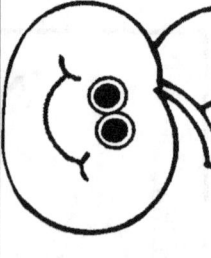

apple 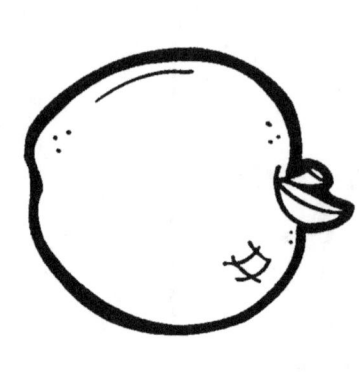	carrot 
pepper 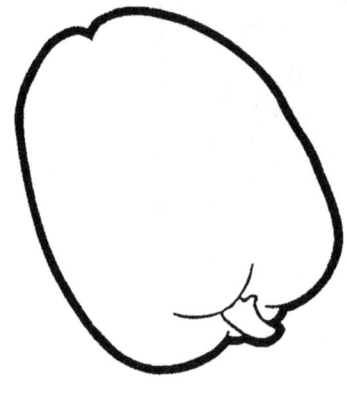	corn 
pineapple 	potato 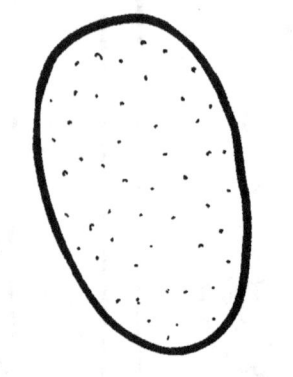
eggplant 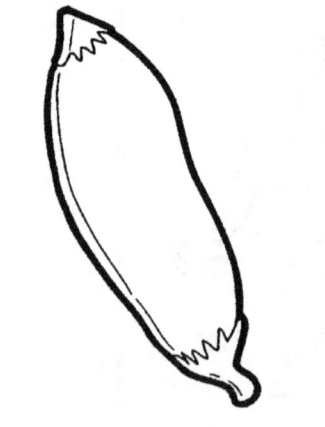	tomato 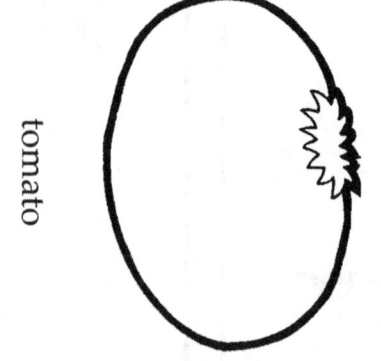

Fruit-Vegetable Bingo

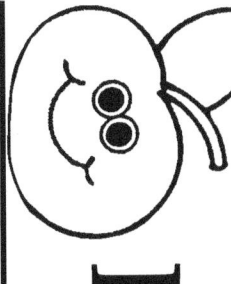

cabbage

squash

tomato

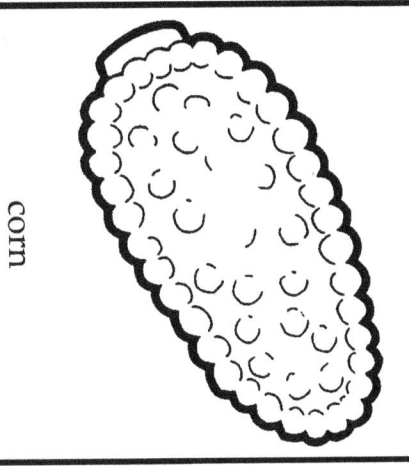
corn

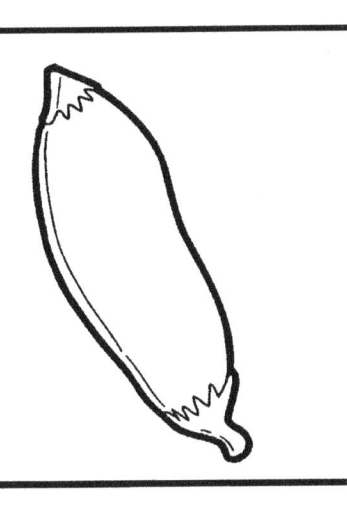
eggplant

pineapple

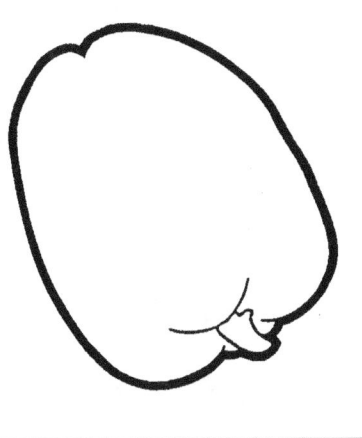
pepper

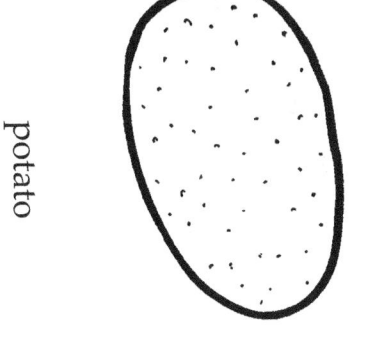
potato

Fruit-Vegetable Bingo

orange	cabbage	tomato	banana
pineapple	squash	corn	pepper

Fruit-Vegetable Bingo

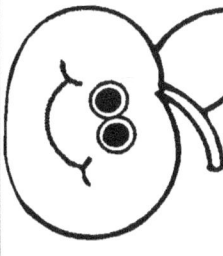

pineapple 	orange 
pepper 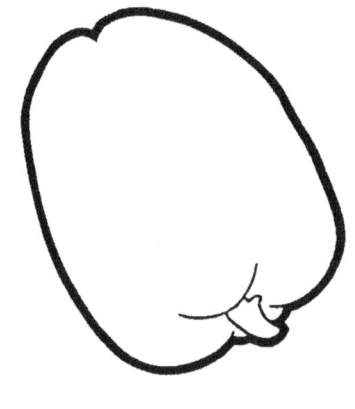	banana 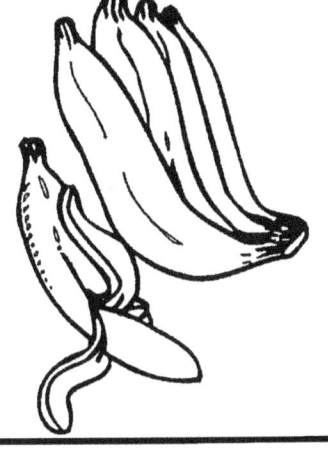
apple 	tomato 
cabbage 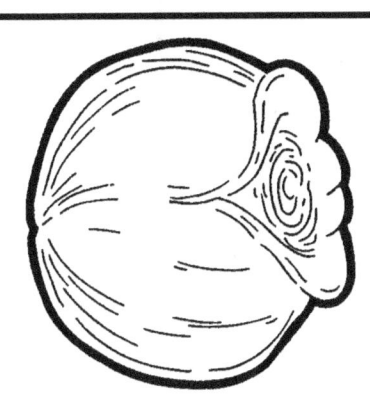	squash 

Fruit-Vegetable Bingo

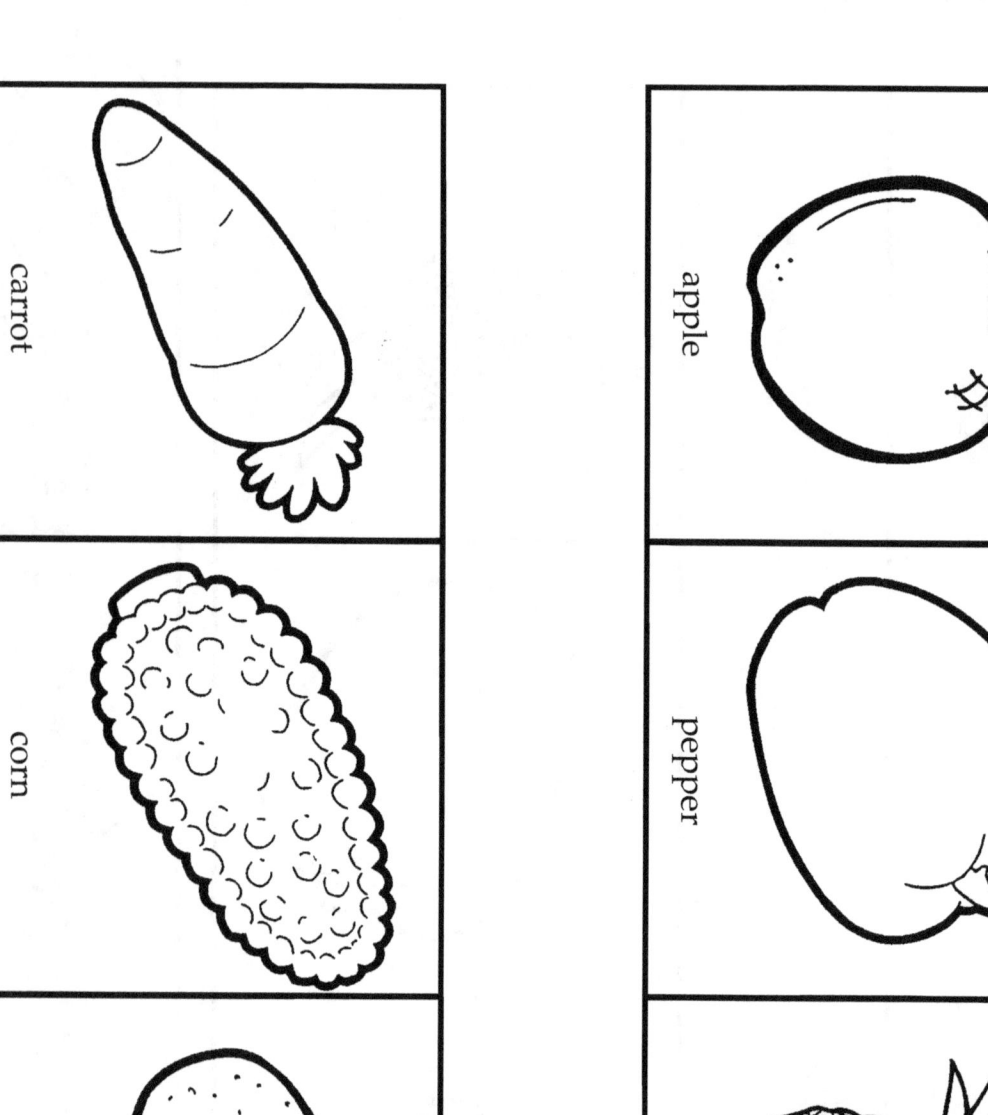

- apple
- pepper
- pineapple
- eggplant
- carrot
- corn
- potato
- tomato

Fruit-Vegetable Bingo

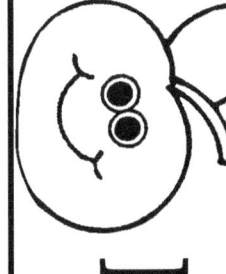

apple 	pepper 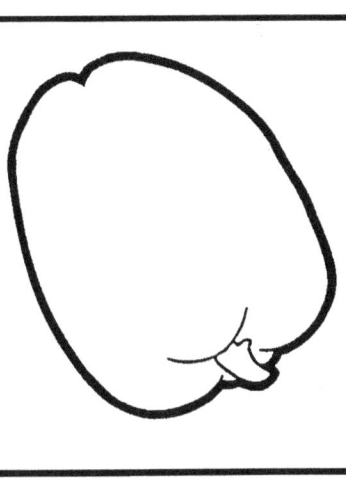
orange 	squash 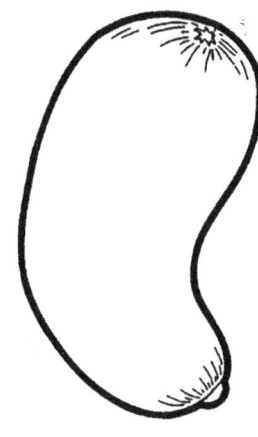
corn 	potato 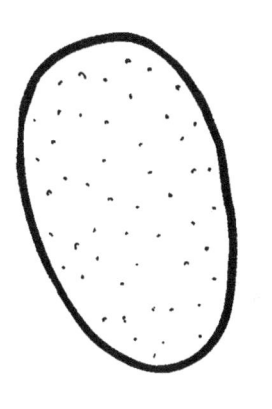
carrot 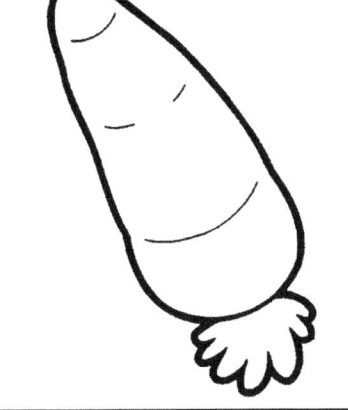	tomato 

Fruit-Vegetable Bingo

corn	carrot	orange	tomato
pepper	apple	potato	eggplant

Let's Eat Out

Get It Together

- Restaurant menus.

- Magazines with pictures of food.

- Construction paper.

- Scissors.

- Glue.

- Aprons for waiters and waitresses.

- Small paper pads, pens, and pencils.

- Restaurant area, created in dramatic play area.

Let's Get Started

- Share a real restaurant menu with the class.

- Discuss eating out. Explain how the cooks, waiters/waitresses, dishwashers, hostess, and cashier are all responsible for running the restaurant.

- Discuss foods that people eat at breakfast, lunch and dinner.

- Have children find pictures of foods in magazines and ask them to cut them out. They can also draw their favorite foods.

- Children sort pictures by the type of meal: breakfast, lunch and dinner.

- Children create their own menus by gluing the pictures on the construction paper.

- Place the new menus in the restaurant section of the dramatic play area.

- Children read menus as they pretend to be customers, waiters, cooks, and hostesses in the restaurant.

Mind Stretchers

- For the developmentally young learner sort plastic foods or pictures of food by fruits, vegetables, and meat.

- For more advanced learners have them decorate cookies to "sell" in their restaurant, using icing and sprinkles (cut out "cookies" from various pieces of construction paper, and decorate using yarn, glitter, etc.).

Teacher Tips

Some children eat the same things for breakfast, lunch, and dinner. It is acceptable for children to list the same food under each category. Be accepting of their food choices.

Appendices

Appendix I
Letter Appendix

Remember to use these letters as models for the letter of the week activity. Adults should trace and cut out the letters for the children

Remember that this is not designed to be a cutting activity for the students. It is also important that the adults cut out the letters to insure that a proper example is provided for the students. When placing the letter in front of the child, be sure that the letter is placed correctly (not backward or upside down). Before the children glue the objects on the letter make sure it is placed correctly.

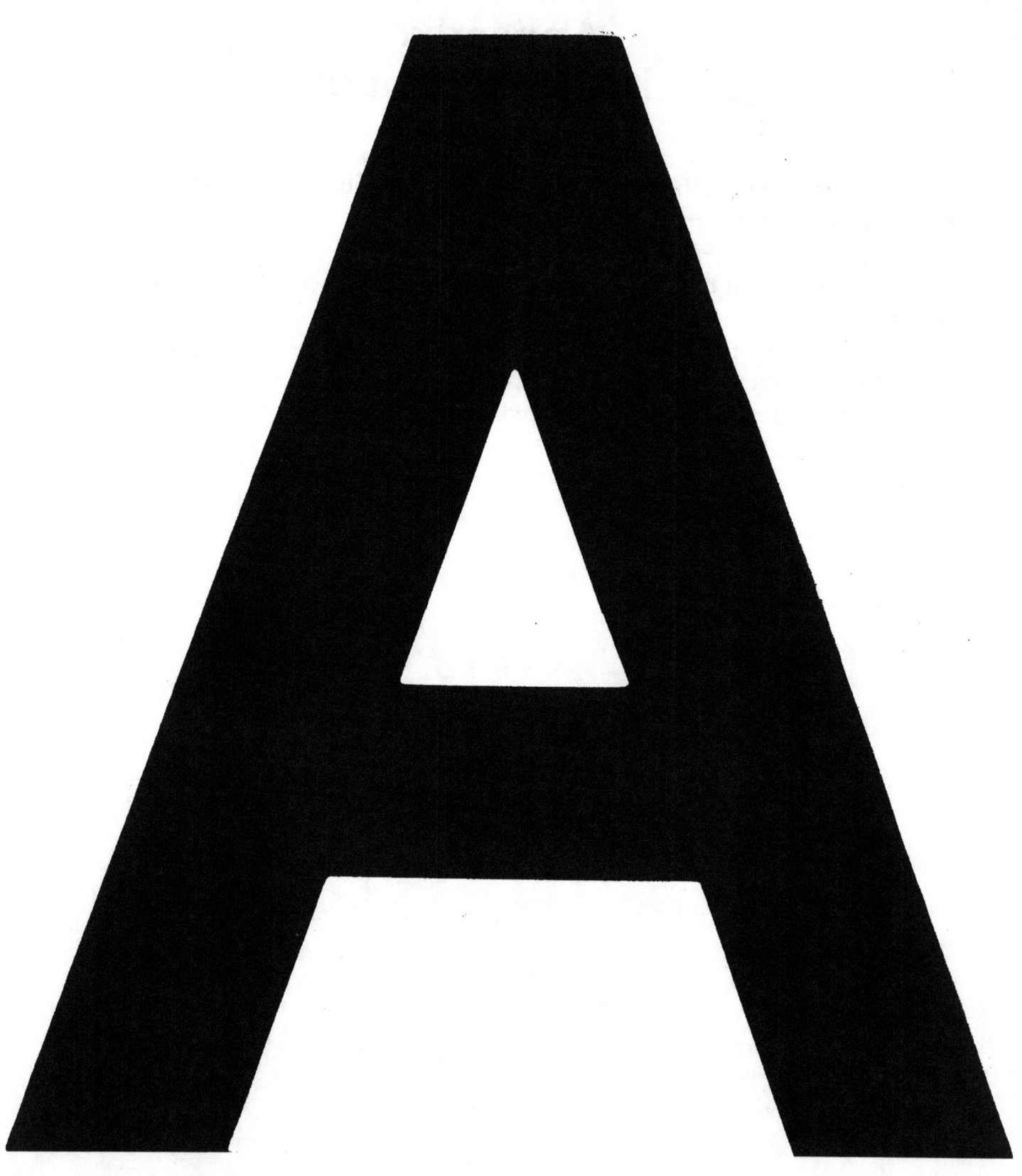

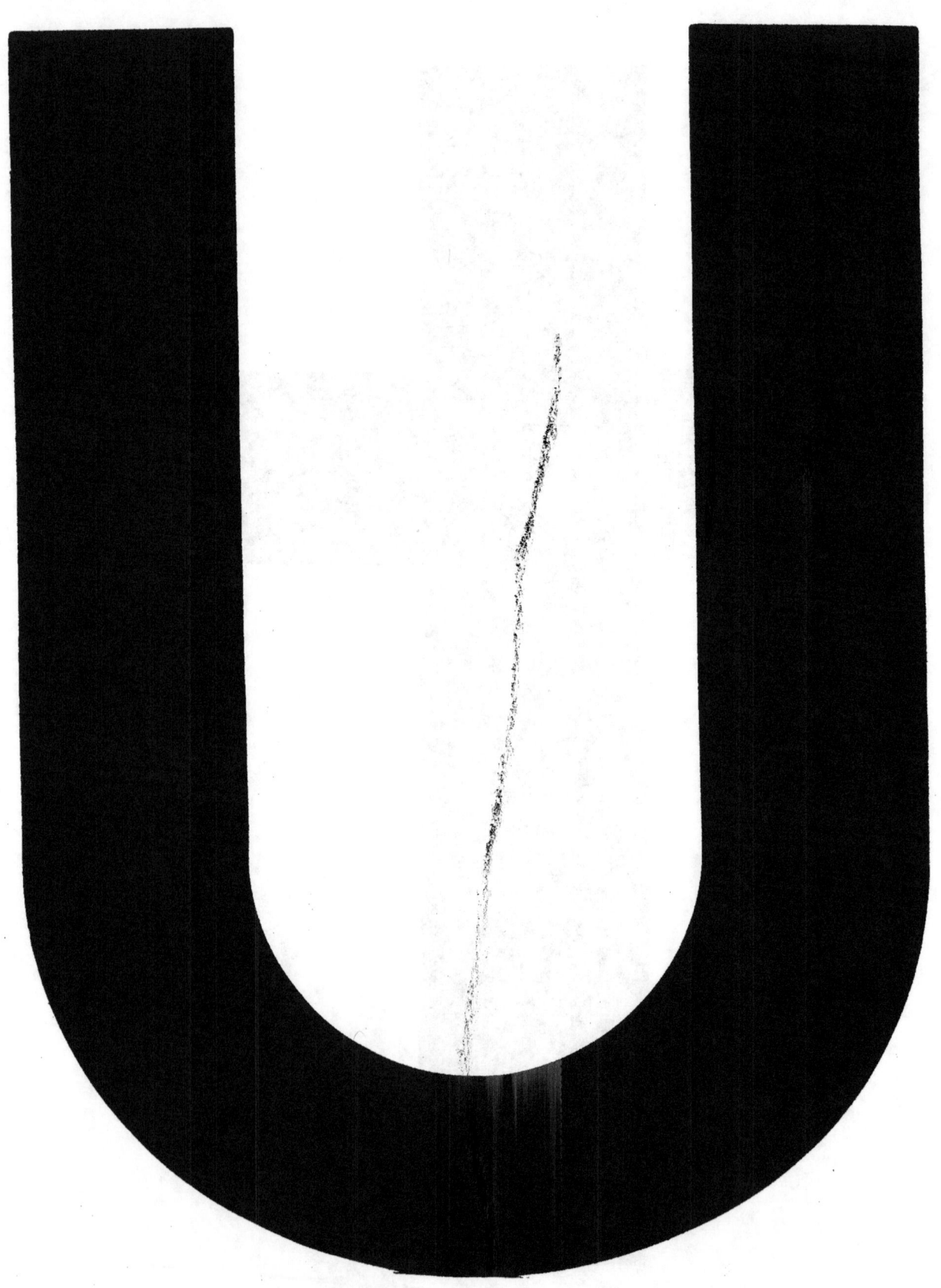

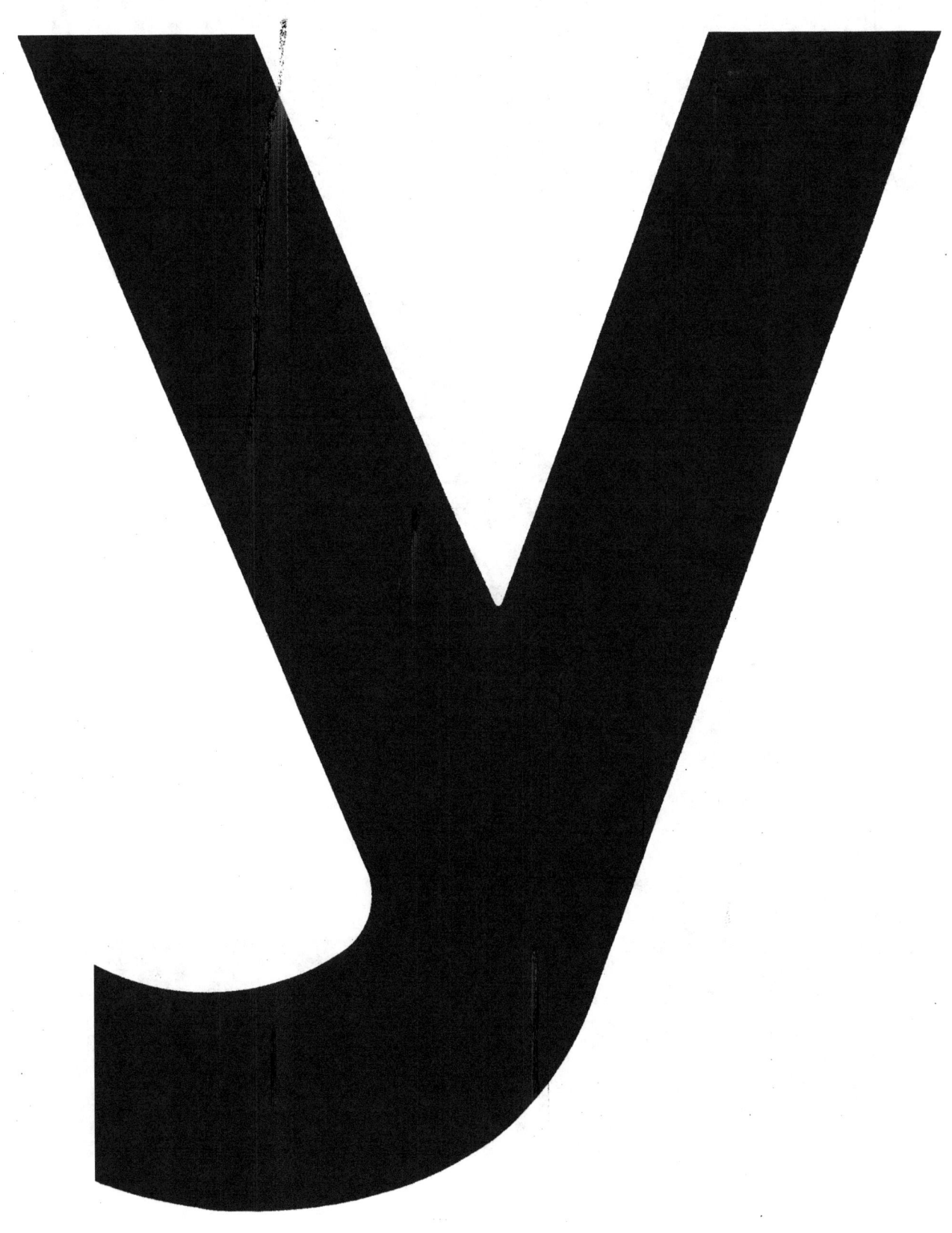

Appendix II
Activity Compliance with Pre-K Standards

The following standards are based upon Voluntary Pre-Kindergarten standards for the State of Florida. Although these standards are specific to the State of Florida, they incorporate the necessary skills to meet the criteria for all developmentally appropriate Early Childhood settings.

I. Physical Health	Where the Butterflies Grow, p. 52	I'm Going to be a Police Officer, p. 53	Alphabears, p. 54	The Bear's Toothache, p. 55	Chrysanthemum	Humpty Dumpty, p. 57	If You Give a Mouse a Cookie, p. 58	I Want to be an Astronaut, p. 59	Pet Show, p. 60	Trucks, p. 62	Harry the Dirty Dog, p. 63	The Snowman, p. 69	Ira Sleeps Over, p. 70	The Little Red Hen, p. 71	A Letter to Amy, p. 73	Gone Fishing, p. 74	Have You Seen Bugs, p. 80
A. Physical Health																	
1. Shows characteristics of good health to facilitate learning.	X	X	X	X	X		X	X	X	X	X	X	X	X	X	X	X
2. Demonstrates visual ability to facilitate learning.	X	X	X	X	X		X	X	X	X	X	X	X	X	X	X	X
3. Exhibits auditory ability to facilitate learning.	X	X	X	X	X		X	X	X	X	X	X	X	X	X	X	X
4. Performs oral hygiene routines.						X											
5. Shows familiarity with the role of a primary health care provider.						X											
B. Knowledge of Wellness																	
1. Shows that basic physical needs are met.					X	X											
2. Follows basic health and safety rules.						X											
3. Participates in physical fitness activities.																	
4. Makes wise food choices.																X	
5. Performs some self-care tasks independently.																	

I. Physical Health

	Clifford's Birthday Party, p. 82	I Am Me, p. 84	The Kissing Hand, p. 86	The Grouchy Ladybug, p. 88	There's an Alligator Under my Bed, p. 91	The Very Hungry Caterpillar, p. 92	Mary Wore Her Red Dress, p. 96	Here are my Hands, p. 97	Twinkle, Twinkle Little Star, p. 99	A Shape for Me, p. 102	Tearing a Rainbow, p. 104	Tear it Up, p. 106	Shape it Up, p. 108	Stop, Drop & Roll, p. 111	Oobleck Activities, p. 113	Mouse House, p. 116	Germy Germs, p. 117
A. Physical Health																	
1. Shows characteristics of good health to facilitate learning.	X	X	X	X	X	X	X	X	X		X		X	X	X		X
2. Demonstrates visual ability to facilitate learning.	X	X	X	X	X	X	X	X	X	X	X	X	X	X	X	X	X
3. Exhibits auditory ability to facilitate learning.	X	X	X	X	X	X	X	X	X	X	X	X	X	X	X	X	X
4. Performs oral hygiene routines.																	X
5. Shows familiarity with the role of a primary health care provider.																	
B. Knowledge of Wellness																	
1. Shows that basic physical needs are met.																	X
2. Follows basic health and safety rules.														X			X
3. Participates in physical fitness activities.																	X
4. Makes wise food choices.																	
5. Performs some self-care tasks independently.																	X

I. Physical Health	Eight Germs, p. 119	Doctor, Doctor, p. 122	Create Your Own Germ, p. 124	Cover Your Sneeze, p. 128	Clear for Landing, p. 130	Astronaut Training Center, p. 132	Big, Small, Big Small, p. 134	I Can Write, p. 136	Look What I Can Do Now!, p. 138	Our Favorite Colors, p. 140	Necklace For My Secret Pal, p. 142	Share a Brush, p. 145	Invent an Insect, p. 147	What is Living in my Pond, p. 149	Musical Share a Chair, p. 151	Look at Beautiful Me, p. 152	Little Boy Blue, p. 155
A. Physical Health																	
1. Shows characteristics of good health to facilitate learning.	X	X	X	X	X	X	X	X	X	X	X	X	X	X	X	X	X
2. Demonstrates visual ability to facilitate learning.	X	X	X	X	X	X	X	X	X	X	X	X	X	X	X	X	X
3. Exhibits auditory ability to facilitate learning.	X	X	X	X	X	X	X	X	X	X	X	X	X	X	X	X	X
4. Performs oral hygiene routines.			X	X													
5. Shows familiarity with the role of a primary health care provider.		X	X	X													
B. Knowledge of Wellness																	
1. Shows that basic physical needs are met.	X	X		X	X	X	X	X		X	X	X	X	X	X	X	X
2. Follows basic health and safety rules.		X															
3. Participates in physical fitness activities.						X											
4. Makes wise food choices.																	
5. Performs some self-care tasks independently.	X																

I. Physical Health

	Let It Melt, p. 158	Healthy Apples, p. 160	Fruit Vegetable Bingo, P. 164	Let Us Eat Out, P. 165
A. Physical Health				
1. Shows characteristics of good health to facilitate learning.	X	X	X	X
2. Demonstrates visual ability to facilitate learning.	X	X	X	X
3. Exhibits auditory ability to facilitate learning.	X	X	X	X
4. Performs oral hygiene routines.				
5. Shows familiarity with the role of a primary health care provider.				
B. Knowledge of Wellness				
1. Shows that basic physical needs are met.	X	X	X	X
2. Follows basic health and safety rules.				
3. Participates in physical fitness activities.				
4. Makes wise food choices.			X	X
5. Performs some self-care tasks independently.				

II. Approaches to Learning

	Where the Butterflies Grow, p. 52	I'm Going to be a Police Office, p. 53	Alphabears, p. 54	The Bear's Toothache, p. 55	Chrysanthemum	Humpty Dumpty, p. 57	If You Give a Mouse a Cookie, p. 58	I Want to be an Astronaut, p. 59	Pet Show, p. 60	Trucks, p. 62	Harry the Dirty Dog, p. 63	The Snowman, p. 69	Ira Sleeps Over, p. 70	The Little Red Hen, p. 71	A Letter to Amy, p. 73	Gone Fishing, p. 74	Have You Seen Bugs, p. 80
A. Eagerness and Curiosity 1. Shows eagerness and curiosity as a learner.	X	X	X	X		X		X	X	X	X	X	X	X	X	X	X
B. Persistence 1. Attends to tasks and seeks help when encountering a problem.	X	X	X	X		X		X	X	X	X	X	X	X	X	X	X
C. Creativity and Inventiveness 1. Approaches tasks with flexibility and Inventiveness.	X		X			X		X	X	X	X	X	X	X	X	X	X
D. Planning and Reflection 1. Shows some planning and reflection.	X	X	X	X		X		X	X	X	X	X	X	X	X	X	X

II. Approaches to Learning

	Clifford's Birthday Party, p. 82	I Am Me, p. 84	The Kissing Hand, p. 86	The Grouchy Ladybug, p. 88	There's an Alligator Under my Bed, p. 91	The Very Hungry Caterpillar, p. 92	Mary Wore Her Red Dress, p. 96	Here are my Hands, p. 97	Twinkle, Twinkle Little Star, p. 99	A Shape for Me, p. 102	Tearing a Rainbow, p. 104	Tear it Up, p. 106	Shape it Up, p. 108	Stop, Drop & Roll, p. 111	Oobleck Activities, p. 113	Mouse House, p. 116	Germy Germs, p. 117
A. Eagerness and Curiosity 1. Shows eagerness and curiosity as a learner.	X	X	X	X	X	X	X	X	X	X	X	X	X	X	X	X	X
B. Persistence 1. Attends to tasks and seeks help when encountering a problem.		X	X	X	X	X	X	X	X	X	X	X	X	X	X	X	X
C. Creativity and Inventiveness 1. Approaches tasks with flexibility and Inventiveness.	X	X	X	X	X	X	X	X	X	X	X	X	X	X	X	X	X
D. Planning and Reflection 1. Shows some planning and reflection.	X	X	X	X	X	X	X	X	X	X	X	X	X	X	X	X	X

II. Approaches to Learning

	Eight Germs, p. 119	Doctor, Doctor, p. 122	Create Your Own Germ, p. 124	Cover Your Sneeze, p. 128	Clear for Landing, p. 130	Astronaut Training Center, p. 132	Big, Small, Big Small, p. 134	I Can Write, p. 136	Look What I Can Do Now!, p. 138	Our Favorite Colors, p. 140	Necklace For My Secret Pal, p. 142	Share a Brush, p. 145	Invent an Insect, p. 147	What is Living in my Pond, p. 149	Musical Share a Chair, p. 151	Look at Beautiful Me, p. 152	Little Boy Blue, p. 155
A. Eagerness and Curiosity 1. Shows eagerness and curiosity as a learner.	X	X	X	X	X	X	X	X	X	X	X	X	X	X	X	X	X
B. Persistence 1. Attends to tasks and seeks help when encountering a problem.	X	X	X	X	X	X	X	X	X	X	X	X	X	X	X	X	X
C. Creativity and Inventiveness 1. Approaches tasks with flexibility and Inventiveness.	X	X	X	X	X	X	X	X	X	X	X	X	X	X	X	X	X
D. Planning and Reflection 1. Shows some planning and reflection.	X	X	X	X	X	X	X	X	X	X	X	X	X	X	X	X	X

II. Approaches to Learning

	Let It Melt, p. 158	Healthy Apples, p. 160	Fruit Vegetable Bingo, P. 164	Let Us Eat Out, P. 165
A. Eagerness and Curiosity 1. Shows eagerness and curiosity as a learner.	X	X	X	X
B. Persistence 1. Attends to tasks and seeks help when encountering a problem.	X	X	X	X
C. Creativity and Inventiveness 1. Approaches tasks with flexibility and Inventiveness.	X	X	X	X
D. Planning and Reflection 1. Shows some planning and reflection.	X	X	X	X

III. Social and Emotional Development	Where the Butterflies Grow, p. 52	I'm Going to be a Police Office, p. 53	Alphabears, p. 54	The Bear's Toothache, p. 55	Chrysanthemum	Humpty Dumpty, p. 57	If You Give a Mouse a Cookie, P. 58	I Want to be an Astronaut, p. 59	Pet Show, p. 60	Trucks, p. 62	Harry the Dirty Dog, p. 63	The Snowman, p. 69	Ira Sleeps Over, p. 70	The Little Red Hen, p. 71	A Letter to Amy, p. 73	Gone Fishing, p. 74	Have You Seen Bugs, p. 80
A. Self-Concept																	
1. Demonstrates self-concept.					X				X								
2. Shows some self-direction.																	
B. Self-Control																	
1. Follows simple classroom rules and routines.					X												
2. Uses classroom materials carefully.					X												
3. Manages transition.s																	
C. Relationships with Adults																	
1. Interacts easily with familiar adults.					X				X								
2. Seeks adult assistance appropriately.					X				X								
D. Relationships with Peers																	
1. Interacts easily with one or more children.									X								
2. Develops special friendships.																	
3. Participates in the group life of the class.					X				X								
4. Shows empathy and caring for others					X										X		
E. Social Problem-solving																	
1. Seeks adult help when needed to resolve conflicts.																	

III. Social and Emotional Development

	Clifford's Birthday Party, p. 82	I Am Me, p. 84	The Kissing Hand, p. 86	The Grouchy Ladybug, p. 88	There's an Alligator Under my Bed, p. 91	The Very Hungry Caterpillar, p. 92	Mary Wore Her Red Dress, p. 96	Here are my Hands, p. 97	Twinkle, Twinkle Little Star, p. 99	A Shape for Me, p. 102	Tearing a Rainbow, p. 104	Tear it Up, p. 106	Shape it Up, p. 108	Stop, Drop & Roll, p. 111	Oobleck Activities, p. 113	Mouse House, p. 116	Germy Germs, p. 117
A. Self-Concept																	
1. Demonstrates self-concept.			X	X						X	X	X	X	X	X	X	X
2. Shows some self-direction.										X	X	X	X	X	X	X	X
B. Self-Control																	
1. Follows simple classroom rules and routines.				X						X	X	X	X	X	X	X	X
2. Uses classroom materials carefully.				X						X	X	X	X	X	X	X	X
3. Manages transitions.										X	X	X	X	X	X	X	X
C. Relationships with Adults																	
1. Interacts easily with familiar adults.			X	X							X	X	X	X	X	X	X
2. Seeks adult assistance appropriately.				X						X	X	X	X	X	X	X	X
D. Relationships with Peers																	
1. Interacts easily with one or more children.				X							X	X	X	X			
2. Develops special friendships.											X		X				
3. Participates in the group life of the class.			X	X							X	X	X	X	X	X	X
4. Shows empathy and caring for others.			X											X			X
E. Social Problem-solving																	
1. Seeks adult help when needed to resolve conflicts.											X		X				

III. Social and Emotional Development

	Eight Germs, p. 119	Doctor, Doctor, p. 122	Create Your Own Germ, p. 124	Cover Your Sneeze, p. 128	Clear for Landing, p. 130	Astronaut Training Center, p. 132	Big, Small, Big Small, p. 134	I Can Write, p. 136	Look What I Can Do Now!, p. 138	Our Favorite Colors, p. 140	Necklace For My Secret Pal, p. 142	Share a Brush, p. 145	Invent an Insect, p. 147	What is Living in my Pond, p. 149	Musical Share a Chair, p. 151	Look at Beautiful Me, p. 152	Little Boy Blue, p. 155
A. Self-Concept																	
1. Demonstrates self-concept.	X	X	X	X	X	X	X	X	X	X	X	X	X	X	X	X	X
2. Shows some self-direction.	X	X	X	X	X	X	X	X	X	X	X	X	X	X	X	X	X
B. Self-Control																	
1. Follows simple classroom rules and routines.	X	X	X	X	X	X	X	X	X	X	X	X	X	X	X	X	X
2. Uses classroom materials carefully.	X	X	X	X	X	X	X	X	X	X	X	X	X	X	X	X	X
3. Manages transitions.	X	X	X	X	X	X	X	X	X	X	X	X	X	X	X	X	X
C. Relationships with Adults																	
1. Interacts easily with familiar adults.	X	X	X	X	X	X	X	X	X	X	X	X	X	X	X	X	X
2. Seeks adult assistance appropriately.	X	X	X	X	X	X	X	X	X	X	X	X	X	X	X	X	X
D. Relationships with Peers																	
1. Interacts easily with one or more children.			X									X			X	X	X
2. Develops special friendships.			X								X	X				X	X
3. Participates in the group life of the class.	X	X	X	X	X	X	X	X	X	X	X	X	X	X	X	X	X
4. Shows empathy and caring for others.		X	X	X												X	
E. Social Problem-solving																	
1. Seeks adult help when needed to resolve conflicts.					X							X			X	X	X

III. Social and Emotional Development	Let It Melt, p. 158	Healthy Apples, p. 160	Fruit Vegetable Bingo, P. 164	Let Us Eat Out, P. 165											
A. Self-Concept															
1. Demonstrates self-concept.	X	X	X	X											
2. Shows some self-direction.	X	X	X	X											
B. Self-Control															
1. Follows simple classroom rules and routines.	X	X	X	X											
2. Uses classroom materials carefully.	X	X	X	X											
3. Manages transitions.	X	X	X	X											
C. Relationships with Adults															
1. Interacts easily with familiar adults.	X	X	X	X											
2. Seeks adult assistance appropriately.	X	X	X	X											
D. Relationships with Peers															
1. Interacts easily with one or more children.			X	X											
2. Develops special friendships.															
3. Participates in the group life of the class.	X	X	X	X											
4. Shows empathy and caring for others.															
E. Social Problem-solving															
1. Seeks adult help when needed to resolve conflicts.			X												

IV. Language and Communication

	Where the Butterflies Grow, p. 52	I'm Going to be a Police Officer, p. 53	Alphabears, p. 54	The Bear's Toothache, p. 55	Chrysanthemum	Humpty Dumpty, p. 57	If You Give a Mouse a Cookie, P. 58	I Want to be an Astronaut, p. 59	Pet Show, p. 60	Trucks, p. 62	Harry the Dirty Dog, p. 63	The Snowman, p. 69	Ira Sleeps Over, p. 70	The Little Red Hen, p. 71	A Letter to Amy, p. 73	Gone Fishing, p. 74	Have You Seen Bugs, p. 80
A. Listening																	
1. Gains meaning by listening.	X	X	X	X	X	X	X	X	X	X	X	X	X	X	X	X	X
2. Follows two- and three-step directions.		X			X		X	X	X	X	X		X	X	X	X	X
B. Speaking																	
1. Speaks clearly enough to be understood without contextual clues.						X		X	X	X			X				
C. Vocabulary																	
1. Shows an understanding of words and their meanings.	X	X					X	X	X	X			X				X
2. Uses an expanded vocabulary to describe many objects, actions, and events.	X	X						X	X	X							
D. Sentences and Structure																	
1. Uses age-appropriate grammar in conversations and increasingly complex phrases and sentences.													X				
2. Connects phrases and sentences to build ideas.						X							X				
E. Conversations																	
1. Uses language to express needs and feelings, shares experiences, predicts outcomes, and resolves problems.			X	X	X	X		X	X	X	X	X				X	
2. Initiates, asks questions, and responds to adults and peers in a variety of settings.																	X
3. Uses appropriate language and style for context.									X	X	X				X	X	

IV. Language and Communication

	Clifford's Birthday Party, p. 82	I Am Me, p. 84	The Kissing Hand, p. 86	The Grouchy Ladybug, p. 88	There's an Alligator Under my Bed, p. 91	The Very Hungry Caterpillar, p. 92	Mary Wore Her Red Dress, p. 96	Here are my Hands, p. 97	Twinkle, Twinkle Little Star, p. 99	A Shape for Me, p. 102	Tearing a Rainbow, p. 104	Tear it Up, p. 106	Shape it Up, p. 108	Stop, Drop & Roll, p. 111	Oobleck Activities, p. 113	Mouse House, p. 116	Germy Germs, p. 117
A. Listening																	
1. Gains meaning by listening.	X	X	X	X	X	X	X	X	X	X	X	X	X	X	X	X	X
2. Follows two- and three-step directions.	X	X	X	X	X	X	X	X	X	X	X	X	X	X	X	X	X
B. Speaking																	
1. Speaks clearly enough to be understood without contextual clues.		X		X	X			X	X	X	X	X	X	X	X	X	X
C. Vocabulary																	
1. Shows an understanding of words and their meanings.		X		X	X	X		X	X	X	X	X	X	X	X	X	X
2. Uses an expanded vocabulary to describe many objects, actions, and events.		X		X	X	X		X	X	X	X	X		X	X	X	X
D. Sentences and Structure																	
1. Uses age-appropriate grammar in conversations and increasingly complex phrases and sentences.									X	X	X	X	X	X	X	X	X
2. Connects phrases and sentences to build ideas.					X						X	X	X		X	X	X
E. Conversations																	
1. Uses language to express needs and feelings, share sexperiences, predicts outcomes, and resolves problems.	X	X	X	X	X	X	X	X	X	X	X	X	X	X	X	X	X
2. Initiates, asks questions, and responds to adults and peers in a variety of settings.									X	X	X	X	X	X	X	X	X
3. Uses appropriate language and style for context.		X		X	X	X		X	X	X	X	X	X	X	X	X	X

IV. Language and Communication	Eight Germs, p. 119	Doctor, Doctor, p. 122	Create Your Own Germ, p. 124	Cover Your Sneeze, p. 128	Clear for Landing, p. 130	Astronaut Training Center, p. 132	Big, Small, Big Small, p. 134	I Can Write, p. 136	Look What I Can Do Now!, p. 138	Our Favorite Colors, p. 140	Necklace For My Secret Pal, p. 142	Share a Brush, p. 145	Invent an Insect, p. 147	What is Living in my Pond, p. 149	Musical Share a Chair, p. 151	Look at Beautiful Me, p. 152	Little Boy Blue, p. 155
A. Listening																	
1. Gains meaning by listening.	X	X	X	X	X	X	X	X	X	X	X	X	X	X	X	X	X
2. Follows two- and three-step directions.	X	X	X	X	X	X	X	X	X	X	X	X	X	X	X	X	X
B. Speaking																	
1. Speaks clearly enough to be understood without contextual clues.	X	X	X	X	X	X	X	X	X	X	X	X	X	X	X	X	X
C. Vocabulary																	
1. Shows an understanding of words and their meanings.	X	X	X	X	X	X	X	X	X	X	X	X	X	X	X	X	X
2. Uses an expanded vocabulary to describe many objects, actions, and events.	X	X	X	X	X	X	X	X	X	X	X	X	X	X	X	X	X
D. Sentences and Structure																	
1. Uses age-appropriate grammar in conversations and increasingly complex phrases and sentences.	X	X	X	X	X	X	X	X	X	X	X	X	X	X	X	X	X
2. Connects phrases and sentences to build ideas.	X	X	X	X	X	X	X	X	X	X	X	X	X	X	X	X	X
E. Conversations																	
1. Uses language to express needs and feelings, shares experiences, predicts outcomes, and resolves problems.	X	X	X	X	X	X	X	X	X	X	X	X	X	X	X	X	X
2. Initiates, asks questions, and responds to adults and peers in a variety of settings.	X	X	X	X	X	X	X	X	X	X	X	X	X	X	X	X	X
3. Uses appropriate language and style for context.	X	X	X	X	X	X	X	X	X	X	X	X	X	X	X	X	X

IV. Language and Communication

	Let It Melt, p. 158	Healthy Apples, p. 160	Fruit Vegetable Bingo, P. 164	Let Us Eat Out, P. 165												
A. Listening																
1. Gains meaning by listening.	X	X	X	X												
2. Follows two- and three-step directions.	X	X	X	X												
B. Speaking																
1. Speaks clearly enough to be understood without contextual clues.	X	X	X	X												
C. Vocabulary																
1. Shows an understanding of words and their meanings.	X	X	X	X												
2. Uses an expanded vocabulary to describe many objects, actions, and events.	X	X	X	X												
D. Sentences and Structure																
1. Uses age-appropriate grammar in conversations and increasingly complex phrases and sentences.	X	X	X	X												
2. Connects phrases and sentences to build ideas.	X	X	X	X												
E. Conversations																
1. Uses language to express needs and feelings, shares experiences, predicts outcomes, and resolves problems.	X	X	X	X												
2. Initiates, asks questions, and responds to adults and peers in a variety of settings.	X	X	X	X												
3. Uses appropriate language and style for context.	X	X	X	X												

V. Emergent Literacy

	Where the Butterflies Grow, p. 52	I'm Going to be a Police Office, p. 53	Alphabears, p. 54	The Bear's Toothache, p. 55	Chrysanthemum	Humpty Dumpty, p. 57	If You Give a Mouse a Cookie, p. 58	I Want to be an Astronaut, p. 59	Pet Show, p. 60	Trucks, p. 62	Harry the Dirty Dog, p. 63	The Snowman, p. 69	Ira Sleeps Over, p. 70	The Little Red Hen, p. 71	A Letter to Amy, p. 73	Gone Fishing, p. 74	Have You Seen Bugs, p. 80
A. Emergent Reading																	
1. Shows motivation for reading.	X	X	X	X	X		X	X	X	X	X	X	X	X	X	X	X
2. Shows age-appropriate phonological awareness.																	
3. Shows alphabetic knowledge.			X														
4. Shows understanding of text read aloud.	X	X	X	X	X		X	X	X	X	X	X	X	X	X	X	X
B. Emergent Writing																	
1. Shows motivation to engage in written expression.							X								X		
2. Uses letter-like shapes, symbols, and letters to convey meaning.							X								X		
3. Demonstrates age-appropriate ability to write letters.							X								X		
4. Shows knowledge of structure of written composition.	X				X		X	X	X	X	X		X		X		X

V. Emergent Literacy

	Clifford's Birthday Party, p. 82	I Am Me, p. 84	The Kissing Hand, p. 86	The Grouchy Ladybug, p. 88	There's an Alligator Under my Bed, p. 91	The Very Hungry Caterpillar, p. 92	Mary Wore Her Red Dress, p. 96	Here are my Hands, p. 97	Twinkle, Twinkle Little Star, p. 99	A Shape for Me, p. 102	Tearing a Rainbow, p. 104	Tear it Up, p. 106	Shape it Up, p. 108	Stop, Drop & Roll, p. 111	Oobleck Activities, p. 113	Mouse House, p. 116	Germy Germs, p. 117
A. Emergent Reading																	
1. Shows motivation for reading.	X	X	X	X	X	X	X	X		X							X
2. Shows age-appropriate phonological awareness.						X											
3. Shows alphabetic knowledge.																	
4. Shows understanding of text read aloud.	X	X	X	X	X	X	X	X	X	X		X		X			X
B. Emergent Writing																	
1. Shows motivation to engage in written expression.		X			X												
2. Uses letter-like shapes, symbols, and letters to convey meaning.					X												
3. Demonstrates age-appropriate ability to write letters.					X						X						
4. Shows knowledge of structure of written composition.		X	X		X			X									

V. Emergent Literacy

	Eight Germs, p. 119	Doctor, Doctor, p. 122	Create Your Own Germ, p. 124	Cover Your Sneeze, p. 128	Clear for Landing, p. 130	Astronaut Training Center, p. 132	Big, Small, Big Small, p. 134	I Can Write, p. 136	Look What I Can Do Now!, p. 138	Our Favorite Colors, p. 140	Necklace For My Secret Pal, p. 142	Share a Brush, p. 145	Invent an Insect, p. 147	What is Living in my Pond, p. 149	Musical Share a Chair, p. 151	Look at Beautiful Me, p. 152	Little Boy Blue, p. 155
A. Emergent Reading																	
1. Shows motivation for reading.		X						X	X	X	X	X	X	X		X	
2. Shows age-appropriate phonological awareness.		X	X					X	X	X	X	X	X	X		X	
3. Shows alphabetic knowledge.		X						X	X	X	X	X	X	X		X	
4. Shows understanding of text read aloud.		X	X					X	X	X	X	X	X	X		X	
B. Emergent Writing																	
1. Shows motivation to engage in written expression.		X						X	X			X	X	X			
2. Uses letter-like shapes, symbols, and letters to convey meaning.		X						X	X			X	X	X			
3. Demonstrates age-appropriate ability to write letters.		X						X	X			X	X	X			
4. Shows knowledge of structure of written composition.		X						X	X			X	X	X			

V. Emergent Literacy	Let It Melt, p. 158	Healthy Apples, p. 160	Fruit Vegetable Bingo, P. 164	Let Us Eat Out, P. 165										
A. Emergent Reading														
1. Shows motivation for reading.	X	X	X	X										
2. Shows age-appropriate phonological awareness.	X	X	X	X										
3. Shows alphabetic knowledge.	X	X	X	X										
4. Shows understanding of text read aloud.	X	X	X	X										
B. Emergent Writing														
1. Shows motivation to engage in written expression.	X			X										
2. Uses letter-like shapes, symbols, and letters to convey meaning.				X										
3. Demonstrates age-appropriate ability to write letters.				X										
4. Shows knowledge of structure of written composition.				X										

VI. Cognitive Development and General Knowledge

	Where the Butterflies Grow, p. 52	I'm Going to be a Police Officer, p. 53	Alphabears, p. 54	The Bear's Toothache, p. 55	Chrysanthemum	Humpty Dumpty, p. 57	If You Give a Mouse a Cookie, P. 58	I Want to be an Astronaut, p. 59	Pet Show, p. 60	Trucks, p. 62	Harry the Dirty Dog, p. 63	The Snowman, p. 69	Ira Sleeps Over, p. 70	The Little Red Hen, p. 71	A Letter to Amy, p. 73	Gone Fishing, p. 74	Have You Seen Bugs, p. 80
A. Mathematical Thinking																	
A(a). Mathematical Processes																	
1. Begins to use simple strategies to solve mathematical problems.					X												X
A(b). Patterns, relationships, and functions																	
1. Sorts objects into subgroups that vary by one or two attributes.									X								
2. Recognizes simple patterns and duplicates them.																	
3. Collects and analyzes information (data analysis).					X								X				
A(c). Number and Operations																	
1. Shows beginning understanding of number and quantity.					X											X	X
A(d). Geometry and Spatial Relations																	
1. Begins to recognize and describe the attributes of shapes.																	
2. Shows understanding of and uses several positional words.																	
A(e) Measurement																	
1. Orders, compares, and describes objects according to a single attribute.					X				X								
2. Participates in measuring activities.					X												
B. Scientific Thinking																	
B(a). Inquiry																	
1. Asks questions and uses senses to observe and explore materials and natural phenomena.				X			X										
2. Uses simple tools and equipment for investigation.																	
3. Makes comparisons among objects.				X			X	X					X				
C. Social Studies																	
C(a). People, Past and Present																	
1. Identifies similarities and differences in personal and family characteristics.													X				
C(b). Human Interdependence																	
1. Begins to understand family needs, roles, and relationships.							X						X				
2. Describes some people's jobs and what is required to perform them.		X							X	X				X			
3. Begins to be aware of technology and how it affects life.																	
C(c). Citizenship and Government																	
1. Demonstrates awareness of rules.		X															
2. Shows awareness of what it means to be a leader.																	
C(d). People and Where They Live																	
1. Describes the location of things in the environment.																X	
2. Shows awareness of the environment.											X		X				
D. The Arts																	
D(a). Expression and Representation																	
1. Uses a variety of art materials for tactile experience and exploration.			X					X					X		X		
2. Participates in group music experiences.													X				
3. Participates in creative movement, dance, and drama.	X																
D(b). Understanding and Appreciation																	
1. Responds to artistic creations or events.																	

VI. Cognitive Development and General Knowledge

	Clifford's Birthday Party, p. 82	I Am Me, p. 84	The Kissing Hand, p. 86	The Grouchy Ladybug, p. 88	There's an Alligator Under my Bed, p. 91	The Very Hungry Caterpillar, p. 92	Mary Wore Her Red Dress, p. 96	Here are my Hands, p. 97	Twinkle, Twinkle Little Star, p. 99	A Shape for Me, p. 102	Tearing a Rainbow, p. 104	Tear it Up, p. 106	Shape it Up, p. 108	Stop, Drop & Roll, p. 111	Oobleck Activities, p. 113	Mouse House, p. 116	Germy Germs, p. 117
A. Mathematical Thinking																	
A(a). Mathematical Processes																	
1. Begins to use simple strategies to solve mathematical problems.		X				X				X						X	
A(b). Patterns, relationships, and functions																	
1. Sorts objects into subgroups that vary by one or two attributes.			X			X						X				X	
2. Recognizes simple patterns and duplicates them.									X		X	X					
3. Collects and analyzes information (data analysis).		X				X						X					
A(c). Number and Operations																	
1. Shows beginning understanding of number and quantity.	X	X	X				X						X			X	
A(d). Geometry and Spatial Relations																	
1. Begins to recognize and describe the attributes of shapes.									X	X			X				
2. Shows understanding of and uses several positional words.				X					X	X			X			X	
A(e) Measurement																	
1. Orders, compares, and describes objects according to a single attribute.												X			X	X	
2. Participates in measuring activities.								X							X		
B. Scientific Thinking																	
B(a). Inquiry																	
1. Asks questions and uses senses to observe and explore materials and natural phenomena.						X				X	X	X	X		X		X
2. Uses simple tools and equipment for investigation.											X		X		X		X
3. Makes comparisons among objects.									X		X	X	X		X	X	X
C. Social Studies																	
C(a). People, Past and Present																	
1. Identifies similarities and differences in personal and family characteristics.																	
C(b). Human Interdependence																	
1. Begins to understand family needs, roles, and relationships.			X		X												
2. Describes some people's jobs and what is required to perform them.														X			
3. Begins to be aware of technology and how it affects life.																	
C(c). Citizenship and Government																	
1. Demonstrates awareness of rules.										X	X	X	X		X	X	X
2. Shows awareness of what it means to be a leader.										X							
C(d). People and Where They Live																	
1. Describes the location of things in the environment.					X					X							
2. Shows awareness of the environment.										X					X		X
D. The Arts																	
D(a). Expression and Representation																	
1. Uses a variety of art materials for tactile experience and exploration.				X		X				X		X		X		X	
2. Participates in group music experiences.							X										
3. Participates in creative movement, dance, and drama.							X										
D(b). Understanding and Appreciation																	
1. Responds to artistic creations or events.							X		X	X	X		X			X	

VI. Cognitive Development and General Knowledge

	Eight Germs, p. 119	Doctor, Doctor, p. 122	Create Your Own Germ, p. 124	Cover Your Sneeze, p. 128	Clear for Landing, p. 130	Astronaut Training Center, p. 132	Big, Small, Big Small, p. 134	I Can Write, p. 136	Look What I Can Do Now!, p. 138	Our Favorite Colors, p. 140	Necklace For My Secret Pal, p. 142	Share a Brush, p. 145	Invent an Insect, p. 147	What is Living in my Pond, p. 149	Musical Share a Chair, p. 151	Look at Beautiful Me, p. 152	Little Boy Blue, p. 155
A. Mathematical Thinking																	
A(a). Mathematical Processes																	
1. Begins to use simple strategies to solve mathematical problems.	X						X										
A(b). Patterns, relationships, and functions																	
1. Sorts objects into subgroups that vary by one or two attributes.							X				X						
2. Recognizes simple patterns and duplicates them.																	
3. Collects and analyzes information (data analysis).																	
A(c). Number and Operations																	
1. Shows beginning understanding of number and quantity.	X		X		X							X					
A(d). Geometry and Spatial Relations																	
1. Begins to recognize and describe the attributes of shapes.				X			X				X						
2. Shows understanding of and uses several positional words.	X		X	X	X						X						X
A(e) Measurement																	
1. Orders, compares, and describes objects according to a single attribute.	X				X						X						
2. Participates in measuring activities.	X																
B. Scientific Thinking																	
B(a). Inquiry																	
1. Asks questions and uses senses to observe and explore materials and natural phenomena.		X		X		X			X				X	X			
2. Uses simple tools and equipment for investigation.																	
3. Makes comparisons among objects.									X		X		X	X			
C. Social Studies																	
C(a). People, Past and Present																	
1. Identifies similarities and differences in personal and family characteristics.			X						X	X						X	
C(b). Human Interdependence																	
1. Begins to understand family needs, roles, and relationships.									X								
2. Describes some people's jobs and what is required to perform them.		X	X														X
3. Begins to be aware of technology and how it affects life.																	
C(c). Citizenship and Government																	
1. Demonstrates awareness of rules.	X	X	X		X	X	X	X					X	X		X	
2. Shows awareness of what it means to be a leader.	X	X			X	X											
C(d). People and Where They Live																	
1. Describes the location of things in the environment.																	X
2. Shows awareness of the environment.														X			
D. The Arts																	
D(a). Expression and Representation																	
1. Uses a variety of art materials for tactile experience and exploration.			X				X						X	X			
2. Participates in group music experiences.			X												X		X
3. Participates in creative movement, dance, and drama.					X										X		
D(b). Understanding and Appreciation																	
1. Responds to artistic creations or events.			X	X						X	X	X	X	X		X	

VI. Cognitive Development and General Knowledge

	Let It Melt, p. 158	Healthy Apples, p. 160	Fruit Vegetable Bingo, P. 164	Let Us Eat Out, P. 165
A. Mathematical Thinking				
A(a). Mathematical Processes				
1. Begins to use simple strategies to solve mathematical problems.		X		
A(b). Patterns, relationships, and functions				
1. Sorts objects into subgroups that vary by one or two attributes.				X
2. Recognizes simple patterns and duplicates them.				
3. Collects and analyzes information (data analysis).				
A(c). Number and Operations				
1. Shows beginning understanding of number and quantity.		X		X
A(d). Geometry and Spatial Relations				
1. Begins to recognize and describe the attributes of shapes.				
2. Shows understanding of and uses several positional words.			X	
A(e) Measurement				
1. Orders, compares, and describes objects according to a single attribute.				
2. Participates in measuring activities.				
B. Scientific Thinking				
B(a). Inquiry				
1. Asks questions and uses senses to observe and explore materials and natural phenomena.	X			
2. Uses simple tools and equipment for investigation.	X			
3. Makes comparisons among objects.	X			
C. Social Studies				
C(a). People, Past and Present				
1. Identifies similarities and differences in personal and family characteristics.				
C(b). Human Interdependence				
1. Begins to understand family needs, roles, and relationships.				X
2. Describes some people's jobs and what is required to perform them.				
3. Begins to be aware of technology and how it affects life.				
C(c). Citizenship and Government				
1. Demonstrates awareness of rules.	X	X	X	X
2. Shows awareness of what it means to be a leader.				X
C(d). People and Where They Live				
1. Describes the location of things in the environment.				
2. Shows awareness of the environment.				
D. The Arts				
D(a). Expression and Representation				
1. Uses a variety of art materials for tactile experience and exploration.				
2. Participates in group music experiences.				
3. Participates in creative movement, dance, and drama.				
D(b). Understanding and Appreciation				
1. Responds to artistic creations or events.				

VII. Motor Development

	Where the Butterflies Grow, p. 52	I'm Going to be a Police Office, p. 53	Alphabears, p. 54	The Bear's Toothache, p. 55	Chrysanthemum	Humpty Dumpty, p. 57	If You Give a Mouse a Cookie, p. 58	I Want to be an Astronaut, p. 59	Pet Show, p. 60	Trucks, p. 62	Harry the Dirty Dog, p. 63	The Snowman, p. 69	Ira Sleeps Over, p. 70	The Little Red Hen, p. 71	A Letter to Amy, p. 73	Gone Fishing, p. 74	Have You Seen Bugs, p. 80
A. Gross Motor Development																	
1. Moves with balance and control.																	
2. Coordinates movements to perform simple tasks.																X	
B. Fine Motor Development																	
1. Uses strength and control to perform simple tasks.		X					X	X		X	X	X	X	X			X
2. Uses eye-hand coordination to perform tasks.							X	X		X	X	X	X	X			X
3. Shows beginning control of writing, drawing, and art tools.		X					X	X		X	X		X	X	X		X

VII. Motor Development

	Clifford's Birthday Party, p. 82	I Am Me, p. 84	The Kissing Hand, p. 86	The Grouchy Ladybug, p. 88	There's an Alligator Under my Bed, p. 91	The Very Hungry Caterpillar, p. 92	Mary Wore Her Red Dress, p. 96	Here are my Hands, p. 97	Twinkle, Twinkle Little Star, p. 99	A Shape for Me, p. 102	Tearing a Rainbow, p. 104	Tear it Up, p. 106	Shape it Up, p. 108	Stop, Drop & Roll, p. 111	Oobleck Activities, p. 113	Mouse House, p. 116	Germy Germs, p. 117
A. Gross Motor Development																	
1. Moves with balance and control.							X						X	X	X		
2. Coordinates movements to perform simple tasks.			X			X			X	X			X	X	X		
B. Fine Motor Development																	
1. Uses strength and control to perform simple tasks.	X		X	X	X		X	X		X	X	X	X	X	X	X	X
2. Uses eye-hand coordination to perform tasks.	X			X	X		X	X	X	X	X	X	X	X	X	X	X
3. Shows beginning control of writing, drawing, and art tools.	X			X	X	X			X	X	X		X	X			X

VII. Motor Development

	Eight Germs, p. 119	Doctor, Doctor, p. 122	Create Your Own Germ, p. 124	Cover Your Sneeze, p. 128	Clear for Landing, p. 130	Astronaut Training Center, p. 132	Big, Small, Big Small, p. 134	I Can Write, p. 136	Look What I Can Do Now!, p. 138	Our Favorite Colors, p. 140	Necklace For My Secret Pal, p. 142	Share a Brush, p. 145	Invent an Insect, p. 147	What is Living in my Pond, p. 149	Musical Share a Chair, p. 151	Look at Beautiful Me, p. 152	Little Boy Blue, p. 155
A. Gross Motor Development																	
1. Moves with balance and control.						X									X		
2. Coordinates movements to perform simple tasks.						X									X		
B. Fine Motor Development																	
1. Uses strength and control to perform simple tasks.	X	X	X	X	X		X	X	X	X	X	X	X	X		X	X
2. Uses eye-hand coordination to perform tasks.	X	X	X	X	X		X	X	X	X	X	X	X	X		X	X
3. Shows beginning control of writing, drawing, and art tools.		X	X				X	X	X	X	X	X	X	X		X	X

VII. Motor Development

	Let It Melt, p. 158	Healthy Apples, p. 160	Fruit Vegetable Bingo, P. 164	Let Us Eat Out, P. 165
A. Gross Motor Development				
1. Moves with balance and control.				
2. Coordinates movements to perform simple tasks.				
B. Fine Motor Development				
1. Uses strength and control to perform simple tasks.	X	X	X	X
2. Uses eye-hand coordination to perform tasks.	X	X	X	X
3. Shows beginning control of writing, drawing, and art tools.	X	X		X

Appendix III
Common Core Standards Correlations

National Child Assessment Form
Teaching Terrific Fours and Other Children

This document is a correlation of the skills presented in *Teaching Terrific Fours and Other Children* to the skills that are assessed on the National Child Assessment Form. This assessment form is used to determine whether students are ready both developmentally and intellectually to move into kindergarten. This correlation indicates where the skills that will be assessed are presented in this book. The number of skills presented in the books in this series will increase with an increase in children's ages, development levels, and intellect.

Social Emotional Development

1. Identifies body parts 84-85, 97-98, 128-129, 152-154
2. Shows feeling ....
3. Separates from parents ....
4. Relates to adults 86-87
5. Interacts with children 151
6. Seeks new experiences ....
7. Maintains interest 69, 88-90, 128-129
8. Plays cooperatively 71, 80-81, 88-90, 113-115, 145-146, 151
9. Modulates voice ....
10. Persists in task 92-95
11. Shows pride ....
12. Shows social awareness 111-112, 128-129, 151
13. Protects self 111-112
14. Concerned about fairness 151
15. Demonstrates responsibility 111-112, 128-129, 151
16. Aware of consequences 50
17. Shows creativity 58, 71, 88-90, 104-105, 124-127, 138-141, 147-148
18. Exhibits appropriate values 111-112, 128-129, 151

Language Development

19. Follows directions (simple) 88-90, 111-112, 151
20. Extended listening 63-68, 71, 86-90
21. Follows directions (multiple) 71, 86-87, 92-95
22. Discriminates between words 136-137
23. Labels objects 72, 92-95
24. Speaks informally 90, 147-148, 155-157

25.	Initiates conversation	
26.	Speaks more extensively	138-139
27.	Asks questions	
28.	Uses prepositions	99-100, 132-133, 155-157
29.	Uses adjectives	
30.	Exhibits auditory memory	
31.	Sequencing and retelling	63-68
32.	Exhibits reading interest	58, 69
33.	Knows reading progression	58, 69
34.	Knows alphabet	54
35.	Uses imagination	58-59, 69
36.	Plays roles	52, 71, 122-123, 130-131, 175-176

Cognitive Development

37.	Visual discrimination with colors	63, 68, 71, 86-87, 140-144
38.	Identifies shapes	86-87, 102, 108-110, 142-144
39.	Classifies objects	59-61, 70, 106-107, 175-176
40.	Understands number concepts	86-87, 116, 119-121, 130-131, 160-163
41.	Knows the five senses	102-103
42.	Draws a person (outline)	152-154
43.	Compares length	
44.	Compares size	92-95, 134-135
45.	Understands numbers	116
46.	Detects a pattern	134-145
47.	Understands relative qualities	57, 60-61
48.	Understands numbers	114-115, 120-121
49.	Knows seasons	69
50.	Draws a person (details)	128-129, 152-154
51.	Classifies objects (matching set to use)	74-79
52.	Recognizes fantasy	52, 58, 82-83, 96
53.	Recognizes cause and effect	128-129
54.	Predicts outcomes	158-159

Motor Skills Development

55.	Walks on tiptoes	132
56.	Walks balance board	132-133
57.	Jumps from stool	
58.	Hops on one foot	132-133
59.	Catches ball (12" diameter)	
60.	Throws ball	88-90
61.	Balances on one foot	
62.	Works puzzle (3 pieces)	
63.	Copies a circle and a cross	
64.	Gallops	

65.	Dances	96
66.	Explores space	154-155
67.	Works puzzle (5 pieces)	
68.	Uses scissors	70, 92-95, 102-103, 128-129, 134-135, 140-144, 147-150
69.	Copies letters	53-95, 136-137
70.	Skips	
71.	Catches ball (3-4" diameter)	
72.	Walks backward	

Hygiene and Self-Development

73.	Allows sufficient time for toilet needs	
74.	Dresses self (basic)	
75.	Knows identifying information	
76.	Uses spoon and fork	
77.	Puts things away	
78.	Cleans spills	
79.	Plays actively	
80.	Manages bathroom facilities	55, 117-121, 124-127
81.	Dresses self (buttons and zippers)	
82.	Helps prepare for activity	
83.	Cares for toys	
84.	Cares for possessions	
85.	Tries new food	
86.	Identifies food	164-176
87.	Demonstrates judgment	111-112
88.	Recognizes weather	
89.	Understands travel	
90.	Knows address and telephone number	

Head Start Kindergarten Readiness Assessment
Teaching Terrific Fours and Other Children

This document is a correlation of the skills presented in *Teaching Terrific Fours and Other Children* to the skills that are assessed on the Head Start Readiness Assessment. This assessment form is used to determine whether students are ready both developmentally and intellectually to move into kindergarten. This correlation indicates where the skills that will be assessed are presented in this book. The number of skills presented in the books in this series will increase with an increase in children's ages, development levels, and intellect.

A. Academics

1. Recognizes letters 14-27, 54
2. Recognizes shapes 86-87, 102-103, 108-110
3. Recognizes colors 96, 104-105, 108-110, 140-141, 149-150
4. Counts 10 objects 86-90, 116, 119-121, 130-131
5. Writes own first name 56
6. Can recognize rhyming words 15-17

B. Self-Regulation

1. Comforts self ....
2. Pays attention 151, 158-159, 164-176
3. Controls impulses 151
4. Follow directions 84-85, 97-100, 104-105, 108-110, 138-139, 151-176
5. Negotiates solutions 151
6. Plays cooperatively 69, 88-90, 96, 113-116, 141-146, 149-154, 164-176
7. Participates in circle time 28-37, 52, 62, 136-137, 142-144
8. Handles frustration well ....

C. Social Expression

1. Expresses empathy 28-37, 71-72, 122-123
2. Relates well to adults 47-50
3. Has expressive abilities 52, 59-69, 80-83, 88-89, 99-100, 124-127, 136-143-154
4. Is curious and eager to learn 55, 62, 80-81, 92-95, 158-159, 164-176
5. Expresses needs and wants 28-37
6. Engages in symbolic play 52, 71-72, 88-89, 92-95, 111-112, 175-176

D. Self-Care and Motor Skills

1. Use of small manipulatives 73, 120-123-129, 134-135, 140-144, 147-150, 155-163
2. Has general coordination 52, 106-107, 111-112, 132-133, 151-154
3. Performs basic self-help/self-care tasks 55, 117-121

About the Authors

Dr. AnaLynn Jones-Sample has been in public education for 20 years, including experiences as an elementary teacher, assistant principal, and most recently the Pre-Kindergarten Coordinator for a large school district in Florida.

Mrs. Carol Crownover has been teaching in the Early Childhood field for over 20 years, in both Pre-Kindergarten and Kindergarten classrooms. She is a certified trainer for High Scope, Creative Curriculum, and Beyond Centers and Circle Time. Mrs. Crownover has worked as a resource teacher for a public school Pre-Kindergarten program for the past nine years.

Mrs. Elizabeth Jones has over 30 years of experience teaching in preschool, public schools, and Kindergarten. She has worked extensively with special needs children. She is currently a resource teacher for a public school Pre-Kindergarten program. Mrs. Jones is highly skilled in assessing the classroom environment, as well as student needs.

www.ingramcontent.com/pod-product-compliance
Lightning Source LLC
Chambersburg PA
CBHW081840230426
43669CB00018B/2767